GRACE COOLIDGE

MODERN FIRST LADIES

Lewis L. Gould, Editor

TITLES IN THE SERIES

Lou Henry Hoover: Activist First Lady, Nancy Beck Young

Mamie Doud Eisenhower: The General's First Lady, Marilyn Irvin Holt

Jacqueline Kennedy: First Lady of the New Frontier, Barbara A. Perry

Lady Bird Johnson: Our Environmental First Lady, Lewis L. Gould

Betty Ford: Candor and Courage in the White House, John Robert Greene

Rosalynn Carter: Equal Partner in the White House, Scott Kaufman

Nancy Reagan: On the White House Stage, James G. Benze Jr.

Hillary Rodham Clinton: Polarizing First Lady, Gil Troy

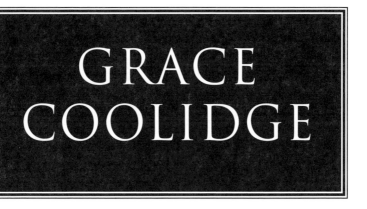

GRACE COOLIDGE

THE PEOPLE'S LADY IN

SILENT CAL'S WHITE HOUSE

ROBERT H. FERRELL

UNIVERSITY PRESS OF KANSAS

© 2008 by the University Press of Kansas

All rights reserved

Published by the University Press of Kansas (Lawrence, Kansas 66045),
which was organized by the Kansas Board of Regents and is operated
and funded by Emporia State University, Fort Hays State University,
Kansas State University, Pittsburg State University, the University
of Kansas, and Wichita State University

Library of Congress Cataloging-in-Publication Data

Ferrell, Robert H.

Grace Coolidge : The People's Lady in Silent Cal's White House /
Robert H. Ferrell.

p. cm. — (Modern first ladies)

Includes bibliographical references and index.

ISBN 978-0-7006-1563-6 (cloth : alk. paper)

1. Coolidge, Grace Goodhue, 1879–1957.

2. Presidents' spouses—United States—Biography.

3. Coolidge, Calvin, 1872–1933. I. Title. II. Series.

E792.1.C6F47 2008

973.91'5092—dc22

2007045737

British Library Cataloguing-in-Publication Data is available.

Printed in the United States of America

10 9 8 7 6 5 4 3 2 1

The paper used in this publication is recycled and contains 50 percent
postconsumer waste. It is acid free and meets the minimum requirements of
the American National Standard for Permanence of Paper for Printed Library
Materials Z39.48–1992.

CONTENTS

Editor's Foreword

vii

Preface

ix

Acknowledgments

xi

CHAPTER 1: Early Years

1

CHAPTER 2: Double Harness

27

CHAPTER 3: "She Took Precedence over Me":
The New First Lady

57

CHAPTER 4: Public Events

77

CHAPTER 5: The Family

96

CHAPTER 6: Together, Alone

121

CHAPTER 7: Later Years

143

{ *Contents* }

Notes

155

Bibliographic Essay

167

Index

177

EDITOR'S FOREWORD

Professor Robert H. Ferrell has written a perceptive and in places very moving study of Grace Coolidge as first lady from 1923 to 1929. Mrs. Coolidge presents significant problems to a student of her life and times. Although she wrote many "round-robin" letters to a close circle of friends, otherwise she was not a discursive correspondent. Her reticent and self-absorbed husband left few traces of his inner feelings toward his wife, and President Coolidge limited her role as a presidential spouse. Despite these difficulties, however, Grace Coolidge was one of the most popular and stylish of the twentieth-century first ladies. With his accustomed skill as a historian and biographer, Ferrell explains how she accomplished all she did despite her less than helpful spouse.

Ferrell is very sensitive to the strains within the Coolidge marriage. His use of the Joel T. Boone papers shows that Calvin Coolidge tested the patience and resolve of his wife and son John on many occasions. There were even moments when the couple might have divorced. Yet Ferrell also recognizes the bonds that held these two people together throughout the politics and cultural life of the 1920s. In that sense, the book is notable for presenting a much more subtle and intelligent look at the Coolidges and their relationship in the public eye.

Even within the constraints that President Coolidge put upon her, Grace Coolidge won over the American public during his presidency. Ferrell shows the public moments when she displayed her natural sensitivity and tact for the White House visitors, guests at ceremonial events, and out and about Washington. The narrative emphasizes her part in the frequent musicales at the White House, which foreshadowed what Jacqueline Kennedy would do a generation later. From Mrs. Coolidge's love of baseball to her support for the Clarke School for the Deaf, Ferrell brings out in a most effective manner the many facets of this thoughtful and sensitive first lady.

The pleasure of reading the book comes from Ferrell's regard for and engagement with his subject. He corresponded briefly with Mrs. Coolidge more than half a century ago, and his esteem for her as a human being pervades the volume. From the insightful portrait of Burlington, Vermont, at the opening of the book to the discussion of the Coolidges and their sons, Ferrell has fresh and perceptive things to say about Mrs. Coolidge. His passing comments on Mrs. Coolidge's predecessors—Edith Wilson and Florence Kling Harding—attest to his mastery of the political environment of the 1920s. Many of Ferrell's passing remarks about the people who inhabited official and unofficial Washington in these years will provoke thought and produce wry amusement. The book manages the difficult feat of being both charming and analytic at the right times. Ferrell will leave readers of this winning volume with the real sense of Grace Coolidge as a human being and a contributor to the historical legacy of presidential wives. Bob Ferrell has made his own unique contribution to the Modern First Ladies series in this very attractive volume.

Lewis L. Gould

PREFACE

This book is about the wife of Calvin Coolidge, first lady of the land in 1923–1929 when her husband was president. It is about how she managed to be his balance wheel in his years of officeholding beginning in 1907, dealing with his nervous, sometimes irascible, temper, making it possible for him to reach—sometimes with some intervention of luck, of good fortune, which all politicians require—the presidency. And how after he became president she lost her influence upon him until in the summer of 1927 he came to his senses and chose to leave the presidency when he could have taken another full term; the marriage triumphed over what he could not have handled by himself. In that sense it is a love story. It appears here for the first time, long after the principals have passed on.

Grace Coolidge made two contributions as first lady. One, the lesser, was her reputation for being among the best-dressed women of her time, virtually the fashion leader of the country. The other was her charm, her ability to meet anyone and make that person feel at home, that the first lady knew that individual as a friend.

I venture a reason for her wondrous hold on the American people, how years after her time in Washington the country remembered her era and her leadership in it. The reason was threefold: her upbringing in gorgeous Burlington, Vermont; the closeness of her family; and finally her belief—she grew up in the high noon of formal religion, the late nineteenth century—that she was a part of God's world and that he would watch over her and guide her life.

ACKNOWLEDGMENTS

My thanks to Mark Stoler of the University of Vermont, who set out the history of Burlington—telling me where to look for the best sources—and did so similarly for the university, and to the many other individuals who helped this book in so many ways. Julie Bartlett, curator of the Coolidge room and its collections at Forbes Library in Northampton, made everything available, including transportation from the library on January days from my hotel to the far end of Main Street. When Julie was working elsewhere, I relied on Elise Bernier-Feeley, who let me bring manuscript boxes into her place of business. Cynthia (Cyndy) Bittinger, Executive Director of the Calvin Coolidge Memorial Foundation at Plymouth Notch, Vermont, a biographer of Grace Coolidge, allowed copying of the full runs of her manuscript collections, which I had seen in part, not full, and otherwise offered much helpful advice. An old friend in Worcester, Charles V. Reynolds Jr., drove to Northampton eight times to run through and make copies of the Therese C. Hills papers and other collections at Forbes.

My thanks to the director of the University Press of Kansas, Fred M. Woodward, who kindly allowed an extension to the time for turning in manuscript and who is always so encouraging to his authors even when they require a little friendly chastisement. And special thanks to the editor of Kansas' Modern First Ladies series, Lewis L. Gould, who when he saw a first draft of this manuscript realized and pointed out that I had written a bit too much about Mrs. Coolidge's husband, the president, perhaps in memory of my biography in the press's American Presidency Series. The resultant changes I trust markedly strengthened the present book. I am much indebted to Susan Schott, assistant director, and to Larisa Martin, production editor. Susan Eklund, copy editor, saw and marked many points that my fairly experienced eye had missed. In her judgments, she was invariably correct.

Two friends in the Indiana University library, David R. Frasier and Jeffrey C. Graf, used the new University Microfilms finding aid for major newspapers for references to Mrs. Coolidge in the *New York Times* and *Washington Post* and printed out pertinent stories. So did Lewis Gould, a remarkable work of helpfulness. I supplemented this material with items from the somewhat more extensive Annie M. Hannay collection in Forbes.

Betty J. Bradbury was the expert word processor.

GRACE
COOLIDGE

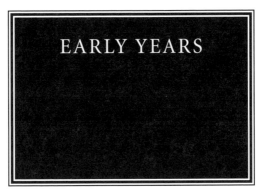

The three guiding forces in the life of Grace Goodhue Coolidge, wife of the thirtieth president of the United States, were the town—city, its residents described it—of Burlington, Vermont; the family in which she grew up; and religion in the institution of the Congregational Church. Born January 3, 1879, when the Civil War was still a vivid national memory, the veterans everywhere, she lived until July 8, 1957, in the era of President Dwight D. Eisenhower, whose army career thrust him into the presidency during a century of world turmoil. Of these enormous changes Grace Coolidge was to become thoroughly aware. But her guiding forces remained from her early years in Burlington, with her tightly knit family and her faith in what she described, in the words of her religious upbringing, as the great white throne.

The town in which she was born was always in her mind. How could it be otherwise? Burlington possessed a beauty that was undeniable. William Dean Howells, when gazing upon the Bay of Naples, remarked that it was the "most beautiful view of the world except one—a Lake Champlain sunset as seen from Burlington."[1] Beauty alone placed the town in the mind of anyone who saw it. The background was the Green Mountains, the foreground the lake, and the vista to the west the distant Adirondacks. The mountains, on both sides, set off the most impressive body of inland water settlers had seen, until moving west they came upon the Great Lakes, and despite the size of the latter none compared with the splendid setting of Champlain. From Burlington, near at hand, the lake revealed Red Rocks, Shelburne Point, Rock Dundee, and Juniper Island, all scenic places that Grace Coolidge and her friends knew well. These they could visit on the steamer *Vermont II,* a squat paddle wheeler with two stacks and a wide fantail. The young girl could cross to these places, else watch the changing shadows of clouds, cast into the lake, as had so many individuals before her: President Martin Van Buren traveled on the steamer *Burlington* in 1840, and Generals Ulysses S. Grant and Philip Sheridan voyaged on the *Vermont II* itself after the Civil War. The splendor of the setting attracted many others. To the north of Burlington, on the Isle La Motte, the young Theodore Roosevelt, avid outdoorsman that he was, attended the annual outing of the Vermont Fish and Game League in 1901 when word came by breathless messenger that President William McKinley had been shot by a gunman in Buffalo. Roosevelt left in a great hurry for the nation's capital to await what might happen, and it did.

Scenery was only part of what the citizens of Burlington took from their gorgeous surroundings, for there was something else, more important: this was Burlington's sense of order. The town did not sprawl but lay in tiers, as if its development had been ordered. It rose on a hill that moved upward for a mile from the shore of the lake. At the top was the university, an impressive place as educational institutions existed at the beginning of the twentieth century; it seemed to have been created all at once, judging from its orderly architecture. Below ran College Street, on which stood a row of fine houses, white in the New England tradition, with green shutters. Spreading from this avenue in suitably straight lines were the other streets, such as Maple, on which the Goodhue family lived. Looking down from the university, one saw a church dome, that of First Church Congregational, and a scattering of steeples belonging to the churches that came thereafter: Unitarian (it had been Second Congregational), Third Congregational, St. Paul's Episcopal, Methodist Episcopal, First Baptist, St. Mary's, R.C. (the cathedral), St. Joseph's, R.C. In the last tier, for the most part not residential, lay the wharfs and nondescript warehouses and sheds of the harbor, protected by a breakwater. The spirit of the times, reflected in the university, dominated from the top, then the houses and churches, and the town's business at the bottom. It was the municipal epitome of order.

The business of Burlington across the years was mainly commerce, the entrepôt for the huge lake that stretched north to south on the state's western border. Founded in 1763, the town benefited from construction of the Champlain Canal connecting the lake with the Hudson River, completed in 1823. Three years later a steamboat company received its charter. For a while grain was the prime export from the wharves, from the state's farms, until opening of the Erie Canal with its bustling lake port of Buffalo, which gave impossible competition to Vermont's farms, many reverting to wilderness. It was all right for the twentieth century's poet to remark about good fences (stone walls) making good neighbors, but he was speaking of the farms of Vermont no longer in cultivation, become sheep farms that themselves were none too flourishing. The stone walls pointed out the barrenness of the soil, for farmers carried the stones to their walls until the farms of the Midwest overwhelmed them. For a while during the years in which Grace Coolidge was in Burlington, the town turned to exporting lumber, also to textiles produced by its cotton mills. But like the farms the lumber trade and the textiles came and went, after which commerce comprised shipment of bulk goods difficult for the state's railroads to carry. The town's economy diminished until little was left except the business brought in by the university, which institution failed to grow as did state-supported institutions elsewhere, and the scenery that brought the tourists in summer and fall and skiers in the Adirondacks and Green Mountains in winter.[2]

Burlington had a few brushes with history, as it did with industry, but like the latter they did not take—which may have been as well, for history often seemed to consume the towns and cities of New England. Near the lake town lay the ruins of Fort Ticonderoga, visited by the young and old for picnics. Within the town was Battery Park, of uncertain provenance, its entrance guarded by two orderly piles of iron cannonballs gathered up, perhaps, or never even used and brought from some ordnance depot to the park. The park did not appear to be an inviting place, judging from its bleak appearance in midwinter, but the cannonballs provided climbing for youngsters who could play at history as they clambered up and down. The

Spanish-American War seems to have touched Vermont more than the Revolution, for Senator Redfield Proctor, the proprietor of Proctorsville and Vermont's "marble king," whose stone products filled cemeteries across the entire United States, had investigated the Spanish policy of reconcentrating, putting in concentration camps, the rebellious people of Cuba and called it to the attention of President McKinley and the lower and upper houses of Congress. One day early in May 1898, the then Grace Anna Goodhue took a festive trip on the *Vermont II* in honor of a native Vermonter, Commodore George Dewey, whose modern warships blew up the antique Spanish squadron in Manila Bay. Shortly before, the battleship *Oregon* left the West Coast and rounded the Horn en route to the American fleet blockading Santiago, and the battleship was commanded by Captain Charles E. Clark, a Vermonter. Beyond the work of these makers of history the people of Vermont chose not to go, and the war went as it came, its advocates said in too much of a hurry. It did not disturb the order that prevailed in Burlington.

The town in Grace Goodhue's day made some efforts at relaxation from its labors to create what the scenery did not provide; in 1900 it boasted the Waubanakee Golf Club, "for the cultivation of vigorous and healthy athletes," and nearby an assemblage of lawn mowers, that is, sheep. There was a Lake Champlain Yacht Club, which possessed a boathouse. The yachts were single-masted sailboats. The town's concern for order, symbolized by its scenery and tiers of settlement, did not permit much relaxation.

It was Burlington, therefore, its extraordinary natural surroundings and the perhaps fortuitous arrangement of the town in tiers, that brought to the young woman Grace Goodhue a feeling for order—thriftiness also, to be sure, and simplicity, and a certain independence (Vermont required several years after the Constitutional Convention in Philadelphia in 1787 to join the Union).

There was the protective quietness, and closeness, which may be the same thing, of the Goodhue family. Grace's early life, through high school, was happy and without complication, save for one event that she never forgot, an accident to her father when she was a small child.

The Goodhues went back nearly to the founding of New England. The earliest forebear came over in 1635 and settled in Ipswich.

The Goodhue grandparents lived in Hancock, New Hampshire, and Grace's father, Andrew Issachar, in the seventh generation, at age eighteen went to Nashua and apprenticed for three years, and there met a pretty, auburn-haired girl named Lemira Barrett. They married in 1870 and moved to Burlington.

From Burlington it was not far to New Hampshire, and the child fondly remembered when the entire Goodhue clan assembled in Hancock for summer reunions. Sundays everyone went to church, and during the hymns the congregation arose and turned to the cabinet organ and choir in the back loft. The grandparents died in 1888 and 1899, and the family did not reassemble for thirty years. In 1929, Mrs. Coolidge went back for the village sesquicentennial and again attended the church. A new organ with shiny gold pipes had been installed near the pulpit, but otherwise everything was the same. Memories welled. "The majority of that little family now sing around the great white throne, but we who were present there sang as I think we had never sung before."[3]

With equal fondness Grace Coolidge remembered the summer visits of her Barrett grandfather. The two, grandfather and grandchild, played with matches in the yard in back. The grandfather told Civil War stories, and the two of them marched around in newspaper hats, carrying a drum and tin horn, to the tune of "Marching through Georgia."

Of her two parents there could be no question where the child obtained her sunny disposition, which was her father, although he never was as buoyantly enthusiastic as was his daughter. Grace's mother was different, and one wonders how the two, father and mother, decided to marry. Perhaps her mother's self-centeredness, as Grace defined it, came out later. The child was devoted to her mother; on this score there could be no question. The husband was devoted, and it is difficult to know what may have been the source of the mother's turning inward and her lack of happiness. In long retrospect the tight and unfortunately inward nature of Lemira Goodhue may have been partly the perception of Grace's later husband the president, who took few pains to hide his dislike of his mother-in-law. He never wished to visit in the Goodhue household, and a stay of more than two days was too much. He felt that any notice that people took of Mrs. Goodhue after he became prominent was

A youthful Grace Anna Goodhue. Courtesy of the Forbes Library,
Northampton, Massachusetts.

due to his own success.[4] She may have felt that way, too, and took it
out on him for being governor of Massachusetts, vice president of
the United States, and president. Grace did her best to counter this
situation and patiently looked after her mother during the years
after her father's death in 1923, when Lemira came down to Northampton and lived in the Coolidge house, one senses hesitantly because of its association with her son-in-law. Mrs. Goodhue visited
the White House once, when Grace's husband was inaugurated for a

full presidential term in 1925. After a physical decline, much of it in the Northampton hospital, she died in October, 1929.

Upon moving to Burlington the Goodhues set up housekeeping on the far side of a brick double house on St. Paul Street, belonging to the owner of the mill in which Andrew Goodhue worked as an engineer. When Grace was between two and three, her father built a house on the lower end of Maple Street, at 123, not far from the mill. In 1899 he built a house of three stories, apple yellow with green shutters, a wide porch, and bay window, typical of the era, a fine but not extravagant house for its time, and there Grace would be married to a red-haired Northampton lawyer, later well known. The address was confusingly similar to that of the earlier house, 312 Maple.[5]

In the first of the houses, the rented one, Grace Goodhue remembered a small bay window in which her mother had the plants. A canary or two sang in the cage nearby. In caring for the house the child did whatever her mother did—she had little utensils in the kitchen and a small sewing basket complete with tiny thimble and scissors. It was said wrongly, she thought, that she could sew buttons before she walked. She walked late because she was a "heavy" child. She went everywhere her mother did. She remembered a story, told by her parents, of how when they visited friends in evenings and she became sleepy, she would be put to bed in the nearby room amid all the coats, recalling Owen Wister's 1902 novel, in which some cowboys as a prank mixed up the infants sleeping while the parents talked, leading to great confusion, but, of course, she never was in such a predicament.

The second of the houses, the first one the family owned, she remembered as vividly as the first because of the improvements that Andrew Goodhue lavished upon it after its construction. The initial one, and it might have been most important, was provision of a bathroom, arranged upstairs by portioning off an unfinished room. Inside, among other conveniences, was a tin tub, with sheathing of painted wood, a great luxury. Later he installed a furnace, eliminating the virtually unheated parts of the house where heat from the wood stove in the sitting room did not reach. The work of Grace's mother lessened, for the house was much cleaner than with the stove that required her father to shake the grate, spreading dust all over the house. Then there was the wiring of the house for electric lights.

The change from coal oil lamps to electricity is something that few Americans today can remember, although the present author recalls it indelibly, the time when President Franklin D. Roosevelt brought lights to a farmhouse in rural Ohio in the 1930s. In Grace Goodhue's case it was a revolutionary change. She had gone away one afternoon and remained for hours, until after dark, when she came home and found the house "ablaze with light from cellar to garret."[6]

The improvements in this second house remained in memory for the rest of her life, but a near-tragic occurrence stood out beyond all other memories of 123 Maple Street.[7] Grace was barely five when it happened. Ever afterward she remembered the look on her mother's face when a message came that her father had been injured at the mill and was being brought home. He arrived on a stretcher, still and quiet. "I listened to all I could hear of the accident and watched every move made by the doctor and those who went in and came out of the bedroom." Kindly neighbors came to heat water and tear up old linen for bandages. Andrew Goodhue had been in the pattern room at the mill, sawing a board with a circular saw, when a knot flew out and struck him on the left side of his face, breaking the bones of his nose and jaw, lacerating his cheek, and damaging the muscles of his eye. Stitches closed the wounds, and bandages held his jaw in place. The doctor told Lemira that Andrew's chances for recovery were excellent "because he was young and strong and had never poisoned his system with strong drink nor tobacco." Little Grace was sent to spend some days with a neighbor around the corner and reluctantly gathered a few of her treasures—a doll, her small broom and carpet sweeper, dustpan and brush—and went away after kissing her mother good night.

Perhaps because of the accident Andrew Goodhue in 1886, together with a friend, William H. Lane, became a partner in a machine shop. An advertisement set out their abilities in detail. "W. H. Lane, Goodhue & Co., Hydraulic Engineers at Pioneer Shops, Lake Street. Contractors for complete systems of Water Works for cities and towns . . . manufacturers of Steam Fire Engines, Pull Machinery, Horse Nail Machinery . . . and all Mill and Machine Supplies." The same year, because of Andrew's business, he was appointed inspector of all passenger vessels with steam boilers in the Lake Champlain transportation district by President Grover Cleveland. Interestingly, in a Republican state Grace's father was a Democrat, although the Cleveland portion of the Democratic Party was as conservative as its Republican opponents. With this appointment the family's head found a pursuit that he enjoyed. Known as Captain Goodhue, he kept the office, even after the machine shop closed in 1898, until he retired from inspections in 1920 when he was seventy-three.

After the accident at the mill, life continued placidly for the remainder of Grace's growing-up years, through high school. Little of moment occurred. She remembered one occasion when she met a boyfriend, a redheaded child named Roy Sturtevant. Grace was accustomed to visit an aunt who had a friend, Mrs. Sturtevant, who had what was known in those days as a "millinery parlor" on the third floor of a building on Tremont Street in Boston. The friend and her little son Roy lived in Reading. In the manner of some childhood experiences Grace recalled what happened in all its details. She visited her aunt alone, for the first time, without her mother, and went to Mrs. Sturtevant's, where she played with Roy. Her mother not being present, she forgot and left her gloves at Roy's house, and his mother sent them home to Burlington. Trying them on, Grace felt something in one of the fingers and pulled it out, to see her first love letter, written of all things on a piece of toilet paper.[8]

Of her schoolteachers she remembered Miss Cornelia C. Underwood, a large, somewhat formidable but gracious woman, who taught first and second grades in a small brick building at the corner of Maple and South Union streets, not far from Grace's house.[9] Grace attended Burlington High School, housed in a square, neoclassical edifice at College and Willard streets, where she took the Latin-scientific course, which included Latin but not Greek and two years of French. She admitted that she was not a brilliant student, for she learned quickly and tended to turn to things that interested her rather than take the fifteen minutes necessary to learn well. When commencement came in the spring of 1897, she was chosen one of the speakers. She wrote out and memorized an essay entitled "Tramp Instinct," about which in later years she could not remember a word, which she concluded was just as well, since she had never traveled beyond Boston and knew nothing of tramps.

Last in the group of influences upon Grace Goodhue that formed the core of her being, in addition to the sense of universal order that came from the town of Burlington with its beautiful setting, and the protective screen of her family that ensured the safety of her years of growing up, was a deep-set belief in God and his all-knowing watchfulness over people everywhere, including herself.

The feeling of many people in the late nineteenth century and the beginning of the twentieth, of living in God's world, is difficult to relate to a generation a hundred years afterward in which churchgoing, attention to organized religion, is languishing, many churches frequented by white-haired old people, pews largely empty. Churches seem almost derelicts, lost in the sea of larger buildings, rarely thought of save in times of unusual need, such as weddings and funerals. Megachurches, as they are called, have appeared in areas of suburban wealth, but their practices seem a light-year removed from the rigid formality of churchgoing in the late nineteenth century and the years down to and after World War I. The megachurches seem alien to individuals who remember the older times or stories of them. They do not fit what happened in the United States a century and more ago when formal religion was a portion of so much of what Americans took part in, and took part in it so naturally that everyone expected the Sabbath not merely to be a time of rest but, an almost inverse activity, of strenuous formal observance.

Grace Coolidge could not remember, or even imagine, a time in which she did not go to church. She did not wear religion on her sleeve but thought church was good for everyone, right for everyone, and when she was in the White House would, if opportunity presented, say so. In the political life of America in the twenty-first century, any expression of religion by a political leader or his wife could appear as an attempt at hypocrisy. But for the wife of the thirtieth president no such thought arose in her own expressions of faith or in her thoughts of people she met on political occasions.

Grace Goodhue Coolidge and people of her time referred to their place of worship as "our church home." Grace thought this should be the norm, everywhere, as necessary for a family as three meals a day. It certainly was so in the Goodhue family. Her father had not been a professed Christian when he married, but not long afterward he joined the Methodist Episcopal church in Burlington and pitched every deck of cards in the house into the kitchen stove. When Grace was a child, growing into adulthood, he was superintendent of the Sunday school at the Methodist church. The church was the center of everything on Sunday, what with Bible school and several services, and the Goodhues attended them all.

For a child the services were tedious. The Bible classes could be embarrassing. The child, perhaps aged six, remembered one class where the leader would point at individuals who recited Bible verses; the pointing finger came ever closer, with Grace in a panic. She was sure the leader would point at her, which mercifully did not happen.

The church was the center of much social as well as religious life, and she remembered the box socials. Women chose to be in one of two groups, older or younger. They brought boxes for two, and the men bidded them in, unaware of the donors. Sometimes the choices were not appreciated, and Grace thought there was undercover trading.

When Grace was sixteen she was attracted to the sermons of the minister of the College Street Congregational Church, and her parents changed to that church home. Absorbed in her concerns and bright young life, they supported her. As her father participated in the Methodist church, he took responsibilities at College Street and was promptly elected deacon. Each Sunday he stood at the center door and shook hands with all who came to worship; if it happened to be wintertime and snowing, he stood with a small whisk broom and brushed the snow off their coats. He became the church handyman, not because the other deacons were unwilling but because most of them were college professors and were better at the spoken word. When anything went awry, especially before church services on Sunday mornings, the call went out for Mr. Goodhue. Grace remembered him frequently taking off his coat and putting on overalls and crawling under the organ to fix the pump, which was run by waterpower. Grace too was an ardent participant, and after she entered college one of her close friends, Ivah W. Gale, a shy young woman from Newport, Vermont, who moved into the Goodhue house to room there, recalled that Sundays were full, as busy as weekdays. The luxury of a college Sunday was not sleeping until noon but until 9:30 or so because church services began at 10:30. Sometimes the roommates stayed for college girls' Bible class and then came home for dinner at 1:00 P.M. Different churches sent a quartet to sing at the hospital on Sunday afternoons, and Grace sang contralto. She would return at 4:00 and was free till 6:30, when she and Ivah started for Christian Endeavor and evening services.[10]

Religious faith carried her through life, to the end. In this she was supported—it would have been a prime matter for discussion, had there been lack of support—by her husband. It is true that Calvin Coolidge did not join the Congregational Church until he became president in 1923. This did not except him from attendance, and he and Grace and their sons, John and Calvin Jr., were visible in Northampton every Sunday morning in the Edwards Congregational Church.

After high school, until her marriage in 1905, Grace Goodhue spent four years at the University of Vermont, from which she graduated in 1902, followed by teaching at the Clarke School for the Deaf in Northampton. It was a time about which only remnants, pieces of memory, are traceable, although the broad outlines of those years are clear. The young woman who became, two and more decades later, the first lady of the land was then without fame of any sort, and little is available about her activities. She received the attention given the average person, which indeed she then seemed to be. She wrote letters, but only a remnant of one, to her friend Ivah Gale, has survived. Years later, in her last months in the White House and first years back in Northampton, she composed a charming autobiography. In the autumn and winter of 1929–1930 the latter portion was published in *American* magazine; the early chapters, considered by the editors of too narrow interest, were not published until 1992.[11] They contained charming references to her years at college and the following three at Clarke when she had become, unknowingly, the country's first professional woman who would rise to the position of first lady. In 1935, among fifty reminiscences by individuals who had known her husband, brought together for *Good Housekeeping* by Mrs. Coolidge, one or two touched on her early life before 1905, and Grace herself in introductory comments repeated a few points in her autobiography.[12] This rather scant record, alas, represents all that we know.

After high school the university naturally attracted her.[13] The buildings of the University of Vermont, on the campus at the top tier of Burlington, with the Green Mountains as a backdrop, were

surprisingly large at the beginning of the twentieth century, as revealed in a photogravure book of Burlington at that time. In an era
when most colleges and universities were just emerging from the insignificance that had contained them since establishment of colleges
in the eighteenth century, Vermont stood almost at the forefront.
Chartered in 1791, the first students graduating in 1804, a tiny institution of no perceptible quality, the university received substantial
buildings after the Civil War. By 1897–1898, it was comparable in size
to some eastern seaboard institutions (in 1898 the university in Burlington enrolled 235 men and 44 women). After that, to be sure, the
University of Vermont languished while the seaboard and midwest-
ern colleges grew tremendously, overtaking and surpassing the Burlington institution. This reflected Vermont's lagging economy, which,
even after construction of the interstate from New York City to Canada in the mid-1960s that turned the state into a summer playground
for people who wished to see rural life and a winter ground for skiers,
did not suffice to support a great seat of learning. But, let it be said,
for a while the university in Burlington showed its promise.

The buildings—with names such as Billings Library, Williams
Science, and Converse Hall—were heavy stone affairs with dormers
and peaks and slate roofs, Romanesque in the style of Victorian
America after the Civil War. The principal ones formed a prospect,
a grand sweep across the top tier of Burlington. They looked down
on a statue of Lafayette, to which led a crisscrossing of sidewalks. A
dormitory for women stood nearby, with a veranda across the
front. Its name, Girls Dormitory, showed its purpose in the days
when feminism was unheard of. The small book of photogravures
of Burlington taken in late autumn 1899 or early spring 1900 contained campus photographs, with trees barren so as to display the
buildings; it showed a scene of coldness, a realistic appearance, for
temperatures in Burlington easily went down to twenty below zero
or colder.[14]

Grace Goodhue entered the university in the fall of 1897 but
withdrew at Thanksgiving on the advice of an oculist and spent part
of the school year with the aunt in Haverhill (who led her to Roy
Sturtevant), the rest at home. She returned in 1898, able to read—
whatever her problem—for courses. One can imagine her as she
strode about the campus. She stood five feet four. She was thin,

never otherwise; when in grade and high school, she believed she was in danger of becoming plump and watched her weight, at a time when friends followed the fashion of appearing like the models of the illustrator Charles Dana Gibson, boyfriends describing them as buxom. Her lithe, small figure may have made her stand out, which was not her intention. Nor did she dress ostentatiously, but wore the uniform of college women of the time. She wore what her friends did, which was long skirts and crisp shirtwaists, large and flowing ties, loosely knotted at the neck. It is possible that her penchant for hats, later so evident, appeared at this time; it was an era when women's hats were huge, even a foot high, baroque concoctions, full of ribbons, combs, and spidery lace, unforgettable if the face under-neath displayed the slightest beauty. Ivah Gale admired Grace's imagination in hats, although she did not testify where her friend wore them.

And what did this young woman learn over the years spent at the impressive university so near at home? By all accounts it was not a great deal. She did not find the place interesting intellectually. It is true that the role of women at the university, while nominally equal to that of men, and with standards for women the same, was not large. The first women were admitted in 1872, just thirty years before Grace graduated. The first woman faculty member was hired after Miss Goodhue's time, and in home economics, a subject that least irritated the male faculty when they contemplated bringing a woman into their midst. In Grace Goodhue's time there was still de-bate over whether university educations might subtract from the numbers of females eligible for marriage, forming a hindrance to the natural instincts of young women. Most of the women gradu-ates became teachers, and when marriage attracted them, they had to give up their appointments. The conservative prejudices of the era did not bother Grace, for her problem was one of disposition. She saw no reason to work hard, whatever the purpose. As she went through high school without much effort, so she passed through the University of Vermont. She did not apply herself—did not aspire to, as her friends put it, become a shark by being a grind. She was not above writing letters in class, and Ivah received one. Grace said it was an English class. Perhaps it was in that class that she prepared an essay—entitled "Life"—that did not require much work. She fluffed

it off, turned it in. Her grade could not have been high. The teacher
returned it with the comment, "I suggest that you refrain from writing on this subject until you have had more experience."[15]

Not much of a student, she admired diversions. On one occasion
she took Ivah's eleven-year-old brother, who was visiting, to class.
The class was a bore, and she sought to poke it up. She brought him
in after most of the students were there, the teacher at his desk. The
students murmured; the teacher chuckled and finally said, "Miss
Goodhue, haven't you heard of the law for the prevention of cruelty
to children?"[16]

In the steady round of classes she always could think of something else to do. One night when all was quiet at home and it was
bedtime, after a dull period of study with her roommate Ivah, she
appeared in coat and hat and said, "We're going coasting." They did,
on her childhood sled recently rediscovered. They went outside and
hopped on. The hill was white with snow, no one around to criticize
them for acting like children. Because of Grace's boredom with the
books and assignments, they repeated the experiment many times.
On one occasion her father came along with a friend, returning
from the Masonic Hall, and the friend said he thought those girls
had better be in bed. Bidding the friend good night, Mr. Goodhue
watched the girls go down the hill.[17]

During Grace's college years, apart from the buildings that impressed her, the classes that occupied some of her energies, and
going down the hill with Ivah on the sled in wintertime, she took
every opportunity to socialize, to reach out in friendship. Her remarkable ability to meet people and enjoy their company dated
from the era of college. She became a joiner. When a sophomore,
she was vice president of her class. She sang in the glee club. She
took part in plays. An out-of-stater from Maryland remembered the
laughter and good humor, the gaiety. The swirl of activities caught
her attention, and she enjoyed them all.

Typical of social life at the university was the description she
placed in her autobiography of sleigh rides of young women and
young men out to an inn miles from the campus where they enjoyed
oyster stew and fixings and danced for an hour or two.[18] The group
hired what was describable as a barge from a local livery stable, and
this conveyance, drawn by two horses, animals arrayed with bells,

took them out. The enterprise was duly chaperoned by adults. The young women sat on benches arranged on either side of the barge, or in the hay thrown into the bottom of the barge. Grace remembered one of these affairs, just before everyone put on coats for the return to Burlington, when the men, as if inspired to do this strange thing at once, began walking around the young women, in a circle. One girl timidly asked, "Why?" It turned out that the men had decided, among themselves, that any one of them who put his arm around a young woman during the return would have to get off and walk, and so they were all exercising in advance of the event.

Life at the University of Vermont was not without pranks, which enlivened the sheer cold of the campus and the chores of preparing for classes.[19] Even at a state university, it turned out, there were compulsory 8:30 A.M. chapel services—compulsory if made somewhat easier by a liberal number of allowable cuts. Faculty members took turns at conducting the chapel exercises, some more interesting than others. One especially dry professor, who taught Latin and looked like Henry W. Longfellow, was noticed to carefully run his hand along the banister as he walked up the stairs to conduct the chapel exercises, and this occasioned a prank of marvelous ingenuity. Someone, unnamed, painted the banister with a bright red color. When the professor walked up, he found himself with a red hand, noticed throughout the chapel session. This led to an inquisition by university authorities, in which every student was hauled on the carpet and asked, "Did you, or did you not, have any part in the transgression under consideration?" To this question one student responded, "No, but I know who had a hand in it."

It was at this time in Grace's life that she helped organize the Vermont Alpha chapter of the national fraternity, as it then was known, no apology to feminism, of Pi Beta Phi. It was the first national sorority for women. She brought the fourteen-student group together in the third-floor attic of her house on Maple Street, which her father finished so she could have meetings there.[20] She was the life of fraternity meetings, always ready to do her part entertaining the crowd. She could sing and play and sometimes recite poetry of her own composition. She served as toastmistress at a banquet. She took the fraternity seriously and attended the national convention in Syracuse in 1901, was first president of the western Massachusetts alumnae club formed in 1910. At a convention in Evanston, Illinois, in 1912, she was elected vice president for Alpha Province, covering the East Coast from Toronto to Florida.

Of all her college experiences the fraternity may have impressed her most, the others dimming as the years passed. A group attended the 1915 convention in Berkeley, California, where she was elected president of Alpha Province. Going out on the train in a special car, she was so impressed with the members of the group that she promised to engage in a continuous round-robin of letters. For her, however, the convention did not last as long as she expected. A sign of what was about to happen, her prominence within Massachusetts and then on the national scene, came when she reached San Francisco and began to enjoy the city and her newfound friends. She received a telegram from her husband relating his nomination as lieutenant governor of Massachusetts and asking her to return for the campaign. But the robins, as Mrs. Coolidge called the group of letter writers, stayed together for forty years, into the 1950s.[21]

In the main, college was fun and classes were not, and it should have been evident in subsequent years. Writers about the wife of the president of the United States were accustomed to relate that she was a college graduate at a time when few young women went to college. True enough, but it was four years of enjoyment, with parties, no effort to be a shark. The meaning of those years academically was insignificant. Grace Coolidge knew that, and when in 1932 she went back to Burlington for her thirtieth reunion, it all seemed remote and strange. She wrote about the proceedings to Ivah. She went up on the train from Northampton. One class member she described as a queer duck. Another possessed a wife who was quaint, as if she just stepped out of a period portrait. One of the attendees, an ophthalmologist, told how he had operated on the eye of the king of Siam. The fraternity house had a large mortgage; someone said it would take $600 a year to run it and keep up payments, a large amount of money in the depression year 1932. During the reunion there was a boat ride. One evening Charlotte—an awful driver—came with her new Pontiac, and they went to a sing on the campus. Grace did not see many people she knew. Her memorable accomplishment was to call on her grade school teacher, Miss Underwood. It was all so long ago.[22]

But to return to the young Grace Goodhue who completed her work at the University of Vermont in 1902. The question was what to do, and she resolved it by entering the training course at the Clarke School for the Deaf in Northampton and teaching there until 1905. In this decision to go to Clarke the influence of Burlington was paramount. She had grown up in the Methodist and Congregational churches, which taught the possibility of a better world, on earth and later. The idea of assisting deaf children fitted this belief. She knew the family of John Lyman Yale at 79 King Street, parallel to Maple. Mrs. Yale took her home when the men brought her father from the mill on a stretcher. John Yale's sister Caroline was principal of the Clarke School.[23] The Yales' daughter June had enrolled in Clarke's normal course and was teaching there. June was accustomed to bringing deaf children home for vacation, and one summer brought Charles Scribner, a scion of the publishing house. When June wished to be away, she called upon Grace to look after the youngster. "So I became interested in the deaf very early for I was only thirteen or fourteen years old then."[24]

Family loyalty did not enter in her decision to go to Clarke. Her mother was against it because her daughter would leave the household. This feeling on the part of Lemira Goodhue welled up again when three years later her daughter broached the subject of and then through her fiancé insisted on marriage, a final separation from Burlington, for in those unenlightened days marriage was deemed permanent.

The decision to teach deaf children at Clarke thrust Grace Goodhue into a dispute regarding pedagogy for the deaf that is worth setting out. Founded in 1867, Clarke was the first school in the United States to teach lipreading and speaking rather than sign language—an important change in the technique of instructing the deaf. In the effort to bring the deaf into society rather than allow them to remain outsiders, the dominant technique in Europe and America was sign language, which traced to the work of a French cleric, the Abbé de l'Epée. It was taken up in England and introduced in the United States by Thomas Gallaudet, who in 1817 established in Hartford the American Asylum for the Education and Instruction of the Deaf and Dumb. Horace Mann took an interest in the deaf, and a Boston school was named for him. Gallaudet's son Edward continued his father's work and headed a sign language institution in Washington established by the Jacksonian politician Amos Kendall, which became the present-day Gallaudet University. Sign language schools appeared in all the New England states. Some were boarding schools, others public, open to all mute children who could get to them.

The Clarke School taught lipreading and speaking—that was the difference. Unlike the limited learning possible through sign language, it opened to students the entire English language, with its hundreds of thousands of words. Lipreading was not unknown in Europe, for Thomas Braidwood taught it successfully in Edinburgh, but he refused to divulge his method, which brought a lucrative income. In Edinburgh, however, this different way of teaching passed by chance to the Bell family and thereby to the Clarke School. The grandfather of the inventor of the telephone, Alexander Graham Bell, had been an actor who, when his luck on the stage ran out, became a prompter. Bell's father, Melville, married a deaf-mute, whom he taught to speak, and lectured and taught visible speech, as he described it, in England and America, giving the Lowell lectures in Boston, where he made possible a visit by his son; Melville emigrated from Scotland to Canada, Alexander to Boston. Like his father, Alexander married a deaf-mute, daughter of a wealthy Cambridge lawyer, Gardiner Greene Hubbard, and like his father taught his wife to speak.

When John Clarke of Northampton offered $50,000 to endow a school for mutes, and after his death left $256,000 to the resultant school, Alexander Graham Bell went to Northampton for some months, and from the outset his advocacy of visible speech dominated the new institution. Bell possessed the same pedagogical zeal as did the younger Gallaudet, and after residence his method prevailed. Grace Goodhue found herself caught up in it.[25]

At the school the young woman from Burlington went through the course of instruction in the oral method, began teaching in the primary department, then the intermediate, and with other intermediate teachers lived in a school dormitory, Baker Hall, that stood next to the house of the school's steward, Robert B. Weir. The latter rented rooms to individuals in Northampton, and one of his roomers was the young lawyer who became president of the United States. One morning Miss Goodhue was out early at the side of the dormitory watering the flowers, and—it became a well-known story—happened to look up and see something she had not seen before. It was the silhouette of a man in a window, standing in a union suit, before a mirror in the bathroom, shaving. He was wearing a derby hat on the back of his head, which made him look comical. He would explain to Miss Goodhue that he possessed an unruly lock of hair that he needed to plaster down each morning, and the bowler was the device that did it. Whatever, upon the sight Miss Goodhue broke out in a gale of laughter. Calvin Coolidge looked down, knew he wished to see more of that young woman, inquired of his landlord who she was and, upon discovering she was a teacher at Clarke, asked how he might make her acquaintance. The steward brought them together, and without much if any ado, which was the Coolidge way, also that of Miss Goodhue, the courtship began.

Accounts of the courtship and marriage always begin with the angularities of the suitor, but let us begin with what was more important, what attracted them and what in the years to come held them together. It was Calvin Coolidge's idealism, the need for service in politics. To individuals who saw only his outside demeanor he was a calculating machine, a politician so schooled in devising what was necessary that he could think of nothing else. It was said of his successor in the presidency, Herbert Hoover, that Hoover was the great engineer, measuring politics with a yardstick to which everything had to yield. Hoover's successor, Franklin D. Roosevelt, was thought to embody all the virtues, including a deep admiration for the Episcopal church to which he had been accustomed at Hyde Park. In fact he told a subordinate that he liked to end his speeches on "the God-stuff"—as cynical an appraisal as any politician ever made. But Calvin Coolidge was an idealist par excellence. He probably always had this quality, bolstered by memory of his mother who died when he was twelve and of his sister Abigail who passed on when she was sixteen. What those searing experiences failed to inculcate was managed by an Amherst College teacher of political philosophy Charles E. Garman, a mystical figure who inspired a generation of students. Garman taught that politics was the glue that held society together and that there could be no higher quality than a young man's devotion to bringing political freedom to individuals who in Europe and

Miss Goodhue around the time she met Calvin Coolidge.
Courtesy of the Forbes Library, Northampton, Massachusetts.

elsewhere had been under the governance of despots. American liberties, he said, could be channeled for the common good. To Grace Goodhue all this made sense. She had her own vein of what at Clarke she might have described as service, teaching children to overcome handicaps, and saw the same idealism in her suitor.

In addition there was the bond of religion. Like his wife, Coolidge attended church. He felt the same sense of divine guidance as she did in 1923 when word came to them, visiting his father at Plymouth Notch, brought by messenger in the middle of the night to the hamlet at the top of a mile-long gorge near Plymouth Junction, that Coolidge was president. The two, husband and wife, knelt in the upstairs bedroom and prayed before going downstairs, where he took the oath administered by his father. Word of this went to the newspapers, for the Coolidges did not hesitate to tell it. That it added to Coolidge's political stock was beyond question. But for them it was the natural thing to do. They did it without embarrassment. For him as for her, religion was at the center of their idealism.

Against these bonds the release of divorce, difficult but not impossible in those days, could not occur. The marriage could not fail. Years later Mrs. Frank W. Stearns, the wife of the department store owner in Boston who first sponsored Coolidge as a coming politician in Massachusetts, told the physician of the presidential yacht *Mayflower*, Dr. Joel T. Boone, who served in the White House, that the marriage was in trouble not long after the Coolidges set up housekeeping in Northampton, the husband's quirks and oddities and temper—more about that later—almost persuading the wife that she could not endure them. There was another time, 1925–1927, when Coolidge was into his full term as president, elected by a landslide, that the marriage headed toward the rocks, this according to Boone, who was Grace Coolidge's confidant as well as physician. On each of these occasions the troubles lessened.

Meanwhile, in the window of the Weir house next to the Clarke dormitory, had appeared the thin young man in the union suit, with the sandy-red hair, white and intense face, blue eyes, shaving in the bathroom mirror and wearing the derby. She had laughed and caught his attention. In their respective ages both were old by Victorian standards of marriage. Born on July 4, 1872, he was thirty-three. She was twenty-six.

For Coolidge it was an unexpected development, but he did not hesitate. At age twenty-nine he had written his father in Plymouth Notch, "You are fortunate that you are not still having me to support. If I ever get a woman someone will have to support her, but I see no need of a wife so long as I have my health." This utilitarian approach vanished as he looked out the window at Miss Goodhue. He seems to have made up his mind at once. This decision, if such it was, assuredly displayed his judgment. At the first opportunity he took her up to the Notch, where she met his grandmother, the redoubtable Sarah Almeda Brewer Coolidge, "Aunt Mede," who was a true New England farmer's wife. She spun and knitted, assisted the sick, and acted as a midwife when a doctor could not attend a childbirth. In Grace Goodhue from Burlington she saw a person of her own sort. To Coolidge's stepmother—his father had remarried after the death of his mother—she said, "That's a likely girl. Why doesn't Calvin marry her?"[26]

One of the first results of the courtship was an amusing situation at Clarke, where the children watched the new man in their teacher's life as he called upon her. A former student who remembered those days said, "We thought she was very nice and the children tried to peep through the crack in the door whenever Mr. Coolidge came for we wanted to see her and her beau." The crack was not big, and they made excuses to pass through the door. The lawyer and the teacher may have sensed all the little eyes looking them over and adjourned meetings to the upstairs reception room. The children spied on them there, and the student remembered that Mr. Coolidge always placed his hat on the floor.[27] This was after their engagement and may not have been his only proceeding in the room.

During the courtship two of Coolidge's traits came to the fore, the one more important than the other. The first was his penuriousness, which unlike what the American public would later conclude, was combined with generosity. After his death Grace Coolidge brought together reminiscences by former officials of his administration and by friends, published in *Good Housekeeping,* and herself told a few stories. One was about the macaroons. Early in the courtship, she said, he heard that she and two friends were planning a picnic and inquired whether he might attend. After consultation with the others it was decided that he could provide the lunch. He agreed and brought two large chicken sandwiches for each picnicker, a divided and buttered shortcake for each, with crushed and sweetened strawberries in a jar, and a dozen macaroons, a substantial lunch even for diners in the early twentieth century. Consuming the entrées and shortcake, the group slowed down on the macaroons. Afterward, picking up the dishes, the provider found that some macaroons remained; he counted those consumed by affirmation of each person present, and half a macaroon was missing. "For it," Grace Coolidge commented, "no account has ever been made."[28]

A second, more serious, trait, evident in the months of getting acquainted, was his silence. Weir remarked it by saying that Grace Goodhue, having taught the deaf to hear, might cause the mute to speak. Soon her suitor's strangely quiet behavior manifested itself. Grace Goodhue took him to see a college classmate who lived in the country and would become, at the marriage, the only bridesmaid, Ethel M. Stevens. On this crucial occasion Coolidge did his best, by his own lights. He came for Grace with a horse and buggy, everything spic and span. In the back she noticed a whisk broom. After arrival he took the equipage to the rear of the house and tied the horse, then devoted the whisk broom to brushing his clothes and shoes. The couple entered the house. Conversation between Grace and Ethel ensued, Coolidge saying nothing. Regardless of what Grace or Ethel did to get him into the conversation, he said nothing, looked straight ahead. He knew he was on exhibit but did not lift a finger to be conversational. Finally he ventured it might be time to go. Afterward Ethel said, "My land, Grace, I'd be afraid of him." Grace protested to Calvin: "Now why did you act like that? She thinks that you are a perfect stick and said she'd be afraid of you." To which he said, with no additional comment, "She'll find out I am human."[29]

When he went up to Burlington and met her parents, his behavior was not much better, in terms of expressing himself, although this time he blurted out what he had in mind. What he said to Lemira Goodhue is unrecorded; she may have sensed that an enemy was entering her household. With the far more genial Captain Goodhue, a little embarrassed over the encounter, the conversation went as follows, after a silence on the part of both men:

"Up here on some law business, Mr. Coolidge?"

"No. Up here to ask your permission to marry Grace."

"Does she know it?"

"No, but she soon will."

A biographer inquired of Ivah Gale years later, after Grace died, whether there was any more inquiry as to Coolidge's ability to express himself. Ivah said there was. Ivah was asked to go out on a buggy ride with Coolidge. Grace wished to know what Ivah thought of him. The drive lasted three hours. Grace told Ivah it might be a quiet affair. Upon return she took her aside, "Well, Ivah, did he talk any?" "Yes," was the answer. "I liked him."[30] It turned out that she admired him for his silence, which was her own way with people—she was a shy girl.

In a letter three days before the wedding Grace wrote Ivah an appraisal, worth quoting, a classic description of one of the outstanding characteristics of the man she married:

> He is quiet and doesn't say much, but what he does say amounts to something. Miss Willoughby was having some work done at the dentist's in Northampton the other day and Dr. Nichols said that he was glad Coolidge was going to get married and he hoped his wife would be somebody who would train him right. He said he didn't talk enough, that people thought him unfriendly when quite the opposite was true. I knew that would amuse Calvin so I wrote him about it and he wrote back that he expected I'd make a great deal better man of him but that he didn't believe I'd ever get him to talking much.[31]

In the weeks before the wedding there was sparring between the fiancé and Mrs. Goodhue, in which the latter lost. Grace told the story in *Good Housekeeping*. "My mother and her son-in-law," she wrote, "did not always see eye to eye."[32] Both, she said, were accustomed to getting their own way. They argued over the date of the marriage. Mrs. Goodhue opined that her daughter should resign from teaching at Clarke and spend a year at home, in preparation, one suspects so the mother could get her hands on her daughter. "Mr. Coolidge," according to Grace (she referred to him formally when writing about him), "took the position that we were both old enough to know our own minds, that he was able to support a wife, and that there was no reason for delay." The argument advanced to a place where her mother held out for November, Coolidge for October. "Eventually he won in the draw."

Preparations for the wedding were uncomplicated. The bride sent out 256 announcements from which she did not expect presents. There were two envelopes for each, and Grace told Ivah, who could not come because she was in Bar Harbor and desired the details, that just before the wedding she had 200 to go. She received a few gifts, such as spoons from her father's family. There was a painted wooden box for dishes. One relative promised a tea set, to be purchased in Northampton. A pair of farm relatives sent five dollars; they could not leave the farm. Among the gifts was one cherished above all others. This was a counterpane knitted by Coolidge's mother during her days of invalidism.[33]

On the evening before the wedding the house filled with friends who came to help with the preparations. One helper arrived late and was decorating and saw a sandy-haired young man who took no part in the cacophony of voices. It was Coolidge, and she asked Mrs. Goodhue: "That young man standing by himself in the corner—is he one of Grace's pupils?"[34]

The ceremony the next day was long remembered. On the groom's side was Coolidge's father and stepmother, and Aunt Sarah Pollard and husband from Proctorsville. Dr. A. H. McCormick, who stood up for the groom, was the latter's general manager, as Grace described him. The groom's guests were the only people from out of town. The minister was Edward Hungerford; the College Street Church was without a pastor, and Hungerford filled in. Dr. McCormick neglected to send a horse and buggy for the minister, who arrived in his own buggy, barely a minute before the ceremony. The groom apparently wore a Prince Albert and top hat; the bride, who wore a gray suit and a high pompadour complete with comb and velvet bow, carried a bouquet of flowers from the Goodhue garden. The couple stood in front of the bay window, around which the decorators made a bower with the vines of a clematis from the front porch. The bride remembered the afternoon sun shining in through the lace curtains.

CHAPTER 2

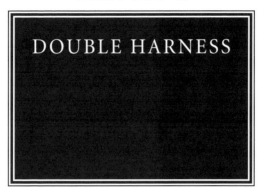

DOUBLE HARNESS

The marriage of Grace Goodhue and Calvin Coolidge ensured the rise of Grace's husband to high public office. It seems impossible that he could have done so without her. He was such an angular representation of New England crotchets, and something needed to be done about them; she was unable to eliminate them, but she could stand by him at social and ceremonial occasions and take the stiffness off them. In their personal relations he was difficult enough to have roused up almost any wife, producing marital crises beyond measure. She tempered them, brought them down to reasonable proportions, meanwhile keeping to herself her own opinions, not letting them make everything worse. As a result, when he entered into a succession of political contests beginning in 1906 and moved forward, not inexorably for his career was none too certain until luck intervened, he had no problems at home; everything at his house in Northampton was in order, if sometimes crankily so because of his own devising. Grace Coolidge managed to promote her husband's abilities, make them possible for the conduct of public affairs. If one looked carefully, her influence was behind him, all the way. From the courtship and engagement and ceremony at the Goodhue house in Burlington, in Northampton at 21 Massasoit Street and the birth and childhood of their sons John and Calvin Jr., into the increasing statewide and

national prominence that led in 1920 to election as vice president
of the United States, in 1921–1923 when she undertook the tasks of
hostess for her husband in Washington: all this required the help
of the wonderfully thoughtful Grace, and in every instance she
gave it.

The marriage turned out to be more intricate and convoluted than
Grace Coolidge suspected. Its full dimensions did not become visible
until the opening in the Library of Congress in 1995 of the memoir of
her physician in the White House, Joel Boone, long after her husband
and she and Boone had passed on. Mrs. Coolidge supported her husband before and during the presidency; there was no question about
that. But the work of doing so was surprisingly difficult.

The first housing arrangement the Coolidges made in Northampton after the wedding was the Norwood Hotel, a nearly defunct hostelry where they rented rooms for three weeks, after which they
moved to the house of a Smith College professor who had to go on
sick leave for a year. They then moved to a fairly sizable side-by-side
house at 21 Massasoit Street, where they were to remain, with time
out for residence in Washington, until 1930. In the latter year they
bought a small estate—they rented all the time in Massasoit Street—
named The Beeches, a large, shingled house with several acres and a
fence and locked gate.[1]

After the hotel the places of residences were altogether different
but until years later and purchase of the estate they were suitably
common, nothing elaborate, as befitted the Coolidge family pocket-
book and belief of the head of the household that the family must
not live beyond its means. The house on Massasoit Street rented for
between $28 and $40 per month; the high figure was during the inflation of 1917–1921, during and after World War I. When Coolidge
became governor of Massachusetts in 1919, his friend Frank Stearns
proposed to buy him a house in Boston, but he refused. Coolidge
never took money from supporters. Stearns sent a check for $5,000,
and Coolidge sent it back, explaining that he thought that if he
could not live within his income (which for the Northampton years
averaged $2,000 a year) he was unsuitable for public employ. Actu-
ally, and contrary to Coolidge's preference, matters financial became

21 Massasoit Street, Northampton, Massachusetts, to which the newly married
Coolidges moved. Courtesy of the Forbes Library, Northampton, Massachusetts.

close in 1907, and he was forced to borrow from his father, for the requirements of officeholding stipulated a fur coat and formal gown
for his wife and a ceremonial cutaway for himself. The crisis passed,
he repaid his father.

The stay in the Norwood made a lasting impression, for a curious
reason. The hostelry was about to close its doors, and in true Coolidge fashion the bargains attainable thereby were irresistible. For
several years the Coolidge sheets, pillowcases, table linen, and plated
silverware bore the mark "Norwood Hotel."

Not much can be said about the professor's house at 5 Crescent
Street in which the couple lived until August 1906. Little has survived about life there save a story or two, one about darning socks,
which Grace's husband evidently thought was the first stage in his
wife's domestication. The story is well known. The house evidently
had a bay window, standard equipment for houses at that time, and
she assumed her role of sitting in the window waiting for her husband to come home from the office. She saw him coming down the
street carrying a russet-colored bag. Upon arrival he revealed its

contents; it was crammed full of men's socks, all needing repair—
she counted them and found fifty-two pairs. She was told there
were more where they came from. As soon as possible she applied
herself, which as she told the story thirty years later, kept her out of
mischief for some time. She asked her husband if he had married
her to get his socks darned, and he replied, seriously, "No, but I find
it mighty handy."[2]

A surviving detail of their life together at that time revealed willingness of the husband to poke fun at his wife. The couple went to a
grocery, where he pointed to tangerines and encouraged her to purchase them. Grace had known them in Burlington as kid-glove
oranges but was uncertain of their name in Northampton and asked
Coolidge, who said, offhandedly, "tautogs." The latter was a New England fish. Grace turned to the proprietor and asked, in her best
housewifely manner, "I would like a dozen tautogs please." She then
recognized her error and asked again, suitably, "A dozen of those,"
pointing. She looked at her husband and caught a trace of a smile in
the corner of his mouth.[3]

The third, and last, residence of the Coolidges for a long time was
Massasoit Street, a side-by-side, with a similar half house attached.
Like the Smith College house it was convenient to Coolidge's law office downtown; he could walk the distance. It was off the road that
led down through the valley to Amherst, where Grace's husband had
spent the early nineties in college; he had not gone far, geographi-
cally. One turned into Massasoit Street, and the house was on the
left, going north.

In the minds of people who observed the principal dwelling of
the Coolidge family, the idea of living in a double house showed the
family's plebeian background. Beyond doubt the half house was not
the palatial dwelling of some Bostonians. Years later the word got
out that the aristocratic Senator Henry Cabot Lodge ("The Lodges
speak only to the Cabots . . .") told a reporter, "Nominate a man who
lives in a two-family house: Massachusetts is not for him!"[4] But life
there was more comfortable than in the residences of many Americans. The inside, down and up, was roomy. Entering from the small
side porch, on a pillar of which an ice card stood in one of the photographs of the place (a square cardboard telling the iceman what to
deliver from his cart or truck), a small hallway containing an upright

piano (Mrs. Coolidge liked to play) led into the living room, followed by the dining room and kitchen. The house had no parlor
(Lodge's house doubtless had several). A stairway went up from the
small area between the living room and dining room to three bedrooms, a long hall at the side. In the bedroom looking out on the
street Mrs. Coolidge gave birth to the boys, who lived there together
while growing up. The center room was for their parents. The room
at the back was for Sophia M. Richardson, who was the family cook
from 1906 to 1915, and for Mrs. Alice Reckahn, who followed. The
house's single bathroom was off the hall between the middle bedroom and that of the cook. For storage there was a spacious attic on
the third floor. Dr. Boone, who in the 1920s went up to Northampton occasionally to care for Mrs. Goodhue and stayed in the front
bedroom, remembered the house well. In his memoirs he admitted
that it was quite a contrast with the Coolidges' second-floor residential area in the White House.[5]

The furnishings were as spare as the house. A visitor remembered
the contents, which were not extraordinary.[6] He was welcomed at
the door by Mrs. Coolidge, who had just been downtown to get
something for the boys' lunch. Entering the living room he saw a
book-strewn table, a rug of standard pattern, framed photographs
of Sir Galahad and of Crawford Notch, a sewing bag, a gramophone
without a lid that, so he noticed, contained no operatic records,
standard in houses of the day. There was bric-a-brac on the sill of
the bay window that had its curtains tied back. Hooks on the hall
wall contained the boys' hats, on the hall floor baseballs, bats, and
gloves. A dog frisked around. In the back, through the dining room,
he glimpsed a gas stove. Over the living room fireplace was a framed
motto with this sentiment:

> A wise old owl lived in an oak.
> The more he saw, the less he spoke.
> The less he spoke, the more he heard.
> Why can't we be like that old bird?

This was the house that provided the scene for the pie story, as
well known as the story of the bag of socks. Mrs. Coolidge liked to
tell it.[7] She prefaced it by admitting, a confession for the wife of a
president, that she was not much of a cook. She added that some of

Grace Coolidge and John, c. 1907.
Courtesy of the Forbes Library, Northampton, Massachusetts.

her recipes were broadcast across the nation. They were about as un-authentic as might have been a recipe of the wife of Senator Lodge. (Years afterward Mrs. Harry S. Truman, not much of a cook for the same reason, she always had domestic help, allowed recipes to be in-flicted upon the nation.) In 1914 or so the Coolidge cook was ill, and Grace filled in and undertook an apple pie, using a recipe from a cookbook. Proud of the result, she served it that evening. From appearance it was everything that could be desired. The family, she said, partook of it without comment. She admitted to herself that the crust was a little tough. That evening two Clarke School friends came to call, and as they were about to leave her husband came into the room and asked if they would like to enjoy a piece of pie. They would. Calvin escorted them into the dining room, where he had set the table, napkins and forks in their places. Devotedly (according to Grace's story) they ate. She watched her husband's impassive face and with the skill that only marriage could discern caught a glimpse of amusement, though never a smile. When finished came the query, no smile because that was not the Vermont way with jokes: "Don't you think the road commissioner would be willing to pay my wife something for her recipe for piecrust?" The friends protested the question, with exclamations concerning the virtues of the pie.[8]

It must have been about this time when Grace Coolidge made biscuits, served them to the family, and her husband dropped one on the floor and, at the precise moment, stamped his foot.

The stories raised eyebrows and deserve the comment either that Coolidge's wife was long suffering or that the two had worked out some sort of relationship wherein each knew how far to go. On her part she enjoyed imitating his Vermont twang.

Everything basically appeared to be all right. Grace Coolidge's shrewd biographer Ishbel Ross, a practiced writer about presidential wives, remarked a little of problems between the Coolidges and assumed that, after a few, husband and wife accustomed themselves and lived happily ever after, in accord with the Victorian prescription that a man is master in his own house. Mrs. Coolidge often reinforced this point by remarking that she admired direction and after her husband's death told an apparent intimate, who spoke to the biographer, that she did not know what to do, he always told her what to do.[9] For a long time she said the right things. "Marriage is the most intricate institution set up by the human race. If it is to be a going concern it must have a head. That head should be the member of the firm who assumes the greater responsibility for its continuance. In general this is the husband."[10]

The full truth is that Grace never adjusted. She tolerated, turned in upon herself (or confessed to her confidant, Boone, sometimes to

Mrs. Stearns), lived probably in memory of what life had been when only her mother was an opponent, her father at hand to temper things, watch her and Ivah go down the hill.

Underneath Calvin Coolidge's quiet, his taciturnity, was anything but that—he was hot-tempered in private, insistent on his way, on occasion thoughtless of his even-tempered wife. He was difficult to live with. The Victorians may have said or written this or that about marriage as an institution, but husbands and wives needed to get along, and Coolidge had no idea how to do it. He had to be persuaded, no easy task when he was angry, and his wife was better at this than anyone he could have known. But to get along with him amounted to incessant watchfulness and infinite patience. Biographers noticed the remark in his autobiography that he was shy; the shyness went back to his time in the Notch when the loneliness of the place, just a few houses and a church and school and cheese factory at the top of a gorge from Plymouth Union, separated him from much of life. He recalled that when people came to call, even residents of the Union, perhaps fifty people in all, and he knew each one, he hated to come down from upstairs and meet them, hated to come down into the kitchen and living room. Shyness had nothing to do with it. The temper was the problem.

Grace Coolidge was uncertain of what had gone into his temper, his temperament. She told Boone the president's grandmother, Aunt Mede, had raised him in absence of his mother, that he did not control his disposition as he should at all times, particularly when under strain. He concentrated on his political career, in particular on composition of speeches, spent all his energy on their content, and when under such strain was impatient and irritable. On such occasions, she said, she was his safety valve and let him blow off. Early in the marriage he would come home from the law office, and when he said everything had gone well, she knew it had not, that he had blown up against the office help or a visitor. When he came home irritated, she knew it had been a good day. She tried to keep away from him when he was angry, letting it all settle down. In the presidency the speeches usually were the bad occasions.[11] The Coolidges' son John, who lived sixty years after his father's death and with whom the mother was very close, had no explanation for his father's angularities, for his Grandfather Coolidge was quite different. Colonel John, so known after bestowal of an honorary colonelcy by one of the Vermont governors, was altogether different from the son the politician. The grandfather, John wrote, was tall, over six feet, swarthy, and in disposition affable, easy to get along with. The president was delicate, of fragile build, and—for whatever reason, said John—highstrung and quick-tempered.[12]

It was in dealing with the sons, John and Calvin Jr., that Grace Coolidge differed completely from the ways of her husband. Here again the usual appraisals, embodied in a story or two, did not get beneath the surface. Everyone knew how the preacher talked about sin, an apocryphal story.[13] Coolidge bedeviled the boys with another preacher story about money. In July 1923, the family were guests of the governor of Maine, along with the other New England governors, and attended church at Poland Spring. The minister gave an excellent sermon on thrift. Frank Stearns had just given young Calvin five dollars, and Calvin spent it. The head of the household wanted to find out what had happened to it and asked Grace what the sermon was, and then John, and neither knew, or so claimed. It was Calvin's turn, and at last in exasperation he said what his father wished to hear, "Aw, spending money."[14] Another time when the boys and their father were walking past the bank on Northampton's Main Street (this story also became well known), he asked them to stop and listen, so they could hear their bank account money working for them. The reason for the stories no longer had much application when he began chiding them—in the early years of the marriage money really was scarce. One must presume that the father enjoyed these inculcations, also presume they did relations with the boys little good. They probably went back to the ways of Grandfather Coolidge at the Notch who watched his money, and followed the Vermont custom that may have gone back to pioneer days wherein he tested each of the Coolidge boys when they were babies by placing five-dollar gold pieces in their hands, and if they grasped them that showed they would be thrifty.

Money was only the beginning of her husband's criticisms of the boys. Calvin Coolidge would criticize them about anything. During the Northampton days he was home only on weekends and part of the time at the law office to catch up on business. The remaining time he needed to rest, and anything that interrupted it was too much—he could not understand the boys' essential activity, the household he thought did not support him. When he was governor, the burdens got on his nerves, especially composition of speeches, and he snapped at the boys. The vice presidency and presidency were worse. One night during the latter he found Calvin Jr. going to bed without saying his prayers and gave the youngster a sermon on that problem. Another he asked John, who wore a pair of new trousers but let them droop, whether there were buttons on them for attaching suspenders—galluses, he doubtless said.[15]

The boys differed in ability to stand up to him. Calvin Jr. was younger and, the father may have sensed, more like him. Calvin had a way of turning his father's wrath with a quip so harmless the father backed off. The older son was something else, for the father moved him into almost open rebellion. John stayed away from him as much as possible, to the dismay of his mother who wanted him around, especially when the head of the household was off the reservation. Calvin looked like the father, John the mother. John actually was a soft individual, like his mother. The two were immensely fond of each other. The father must have seen this closeness when criticizing John and may have come to believe the two were combining against him.

At last matters in the early years improved. During the Northampton years, beginning with nomination and election to the lieutenant governorship in 1915, the striving for office—it was a natural thing, given his belief in service, acquired from the teaching of the mystical Amherst seer, Garman, supported by belief in divine guidance—slackened, for he could move into the governorship. His wife, who had to deal with his weekend incursions, and the boys, who suffered them, saw less of him as he kept ever more to his duties in Boston. Grace Coolidge went in to help lend cheer to his loneliness and give support on social and ceremonial occasions. The boys were alone with their friends: Jack Hills, the son of Therese and Reuben Hills, who lived at 69 Massasoit Street and whose father was a manufacturer of brass hardware; Richard and Stephen Brown, sons of

Dr. Edward W. Brown; and Edward Bacher (pronounced "Baker"), whose father was a Boston and Maine Railroad engineer. When the boys' father and mother were gone, Mrs. Reckahn got their meals or Therese Hills invited them to eat at her house; Mrs. Hills (Hillsy) was a close friend of Grace Coolidge.

The present chapter is no place to detail the rise of Calvin Coolidge, the Northampton lawyer, to the governorship of the Commonwealth of Massachusetts and vice presidency of the United States, save to show its relation to the marriage and how the latter affected that rise. The relationship was immediate and, it is fair to say, decisive, in the sense of making it possible.

The first time Grace Coolidge's husband ran for public office was a special case in the sequence of his attempts at officeholding. For one thing, it was the only contest that he lost. For another, it was closely connected with his marriage. After the ceremony in the Goodhue house in Burlington, and with bags packed, the newlyweds took the train for Montreal, where they expected to spend two weeks of sightseeing, theatergoing, general attention to the quaint city. After a week, having seen everything they believed seeable, Calvin and Grace decided to take the train to Northampton, where they needed to set up housekeeping. They stopped for a day or two in Burlington to pick up some of the bride's belongings.

Afterward Grace Coolidge said her husband invented an excuse for breaking off the trip, that he wanted to get back and show off his prize, but had in mind running for election to the school board. It was his first effort at obtaining a citywide elective office. He lost, perhaps his mind not on the task. In his autobiography he explained that the board was a purely honorary office, which had no attraction, but he was asked to be a candidate and consented and was nominated. To his surprise another Republican entered the race, split the party vote, and elected a Democrat. He was accused of being a politician; he had been a member of the Republican city committee, in 1898 was elected to the common council from ward 2, had been city solicitor. A friend confessed that he, the friend, voted for the Democrat because Coolidge had no children in the schools. "Might give me time," was Coolidge's retort.[16]

The rising Massachusetts politician and wife. This is one of the few
but altogether authentic photographs of Coolidge with a cigar.
Courtesy of the Forbes Library, Northampton, Massachusetts.

A darker analysis of why Coolidge lost the school committee
election is possible, although the Democrat who received the office,
John J. Kennedy, no relation to the family in Boston, pointed out in
Good Housekeeping that Coolidge lost by 94 votes out of 1,700.
Coolidge's widow said she had wanted to go home to Burlington for
Christmas; her husband promised that if he won they would go. She
suspected him of arranging the result.[17]

When Coolidge in 1906 ran for the General Assembly in Boston, representing Northampton, it was a serious effort. It did come at an awkward time, for their son John was born September 6, and Coolidge was running. Northampton was basically a Republican city, but there was no certainty he would win. Meanwhile, the new child was not in happy circumstances, Grace unable to nurse. Nothing suited the child when the husband on January 1, 1907, took the train for Boston and his new duties. At last a neighbor recommended a formula that worked.

Coolidge served two one-year terms in the Assembly (all his Massachusetts elective offices were one-year terms). They required time in Boston and affected his income. He received $750 a year, his law business was practically at a standstill, and he had to borrow from his father. He and Grace managed, and the following three years, 1909, 1910, and 1911, were easier, for in the first he took the year off, the only time from 1907 to 1929 he did not hold office. The next two he was mayor of Northampton. He was home every night.

In 1911 he ran for and was elected to the Massachusetts upper legislative house, the Senate, from Hampshire County, the county of Northampton, and two adjoining counties, and on his political way toward the governorship and the vice presidency. Of the four years he spent as state senator, two were feeling his way, making alliances, gaining support of fellow senators. It was during this time that he gained the friendship of Frank Stearns, who had stopped by to see him about the sewers of Amherst, the town and college. In 1914, when opportunity opened to become president of the Senate, he seized it by taking the train for Boston and gaining support of, among others, Winthrop Murray Crane, one of Massachusetts' U.S. senators (the other was Lodge). Stearns and Crane had different objectives, but they centered on Coolidge. Stearns, like Coolidge an alumnus of Amherst, wished to give the college a chance at the governorship, instead of Harvard, whose graduates regularly ascended to the statehouse; Crane desired to support the Yankees of western Massachusetts against the easterners of the Back Bay represented by Lodge. In his inauguration as Senate president, Coolidge made an address often remarked, which had the virtue of being short and in its first sentence advised his fellow senators to "Do the day's work," his personal injunction for every day of his life. He said a

Making music with son John in the Massasoit Street duplex.
Courtesy of the Forbes Library, Northampton, Massachusetts.

few other things, one being that legislation had gone beyond the
state's needs, but they were forgotten in favor of work. That was
something that the Brahmins had forgotten and that propelled
Coolidge and the Yankees. Coolidge became lieutenant governor
and held the office for three years, reelected for 1917 and 1918. Then
the governorship.

Becoming governor on January 1, 1919, he did two things of importance, one for the commonwealth, the other by chance—it does
not seem to have been his purpose—for himself. When he became
governor, he had the temerity to take on the virtual rat's nest of state
offices, apportioned in 118 departments. He sponsored a bill to re-
duce the departments to 18; it passed, and the reduction did not
harm him politically as his predecessors feared. Then during the
Boston police strike in 1919, a mess in which the mayor vacillated,
the police commissioner (whom Coolidge supported) was defiantly
stiff-necked, the police unexpectedly walked out, minor damage occurred (to the value of $34,000) in the single day the city was with-

out policemen, and when the president of the American Federation of Labor, Samuel Gompers, urged reinstatement of the strikers the governor replied with the telegram telling Gompers there was no right to strike against the public safety. Coolidge may have sent it without thought, then realized, horror-struck, that he probably had committed political suicide because of the policemen's very real troubles that were in general supported by the public. In a time of inflation and disorders across the country, the phrase caught on and made him a national figure, even eliciting a statement of support from President Woodrow Wilson in Washington, a member of the opposition party.[18]

In all this Mrs. Coolidge played her essential part, initially keeping the home fires in Northampton, later years going to Boston to give moral support and accompany her husband to occasions. That she knew what was going on, saw what he was doing, must come as no surprise. She did not tell him, for he was an adamant believer in the notion of a woman's place. She made the usual pretensions that she knew nothing about politics.

Grace Coolidge enjoyed the more frequent trips to Boston, although she could not have enjoyed the place in which her husband and she stayed. Typically, although Stearns thought that when he became governor he should take a house and entertain, Coolidge remained in the same dismal hostelry to which he had repaired in 1907. Years later a biographer looked up his room in the Adams House on Washington Street, listed as Suite 60, third floor center. It was as cheerful as a cell; a traveling man would not have taken it, save as a last resort. It did possess the virtue—important in 1907— of costing one dollar a day. The room abutted an inner courtyard the size of an air shaft. Light came through a half-sized window cut off by a chimney. The bathroom was down the hall. The room had a three-quarter wooden bed that substituted as a reading lounge when Coolidge was there at night.[19] When he became lieutenant governor, he expanded the suite to two rooms, one a living and reception room, in which Grace could receive guests. The expanded suite did have a bathroom, also a telephone from which Grace could call the boys in Northampton and her husband could conduct political business without being heard by hangers-on in the lobby.

Calvin, John, and Calvin Jr. watch Grace roll the dice.
Courtesy of the Forbes Library, Northampton, Massachusetts.

Luncheons and dinners, by herself and with her husband, were exhilarating. Many were in the Copley-Plaza, now as then Boston's premier hotel akin to New York's finest. Once in a while the boys came, as when their father was inaugurated president of the Senate, then lieutenant governor and governor. For the latter occasion the grandfathers came, from Burlington and the Notch. The boys liked the meals, perhaps at the Copley. At one John and Calvin Jr. were presented with whole chickens. Momentarily separated from their parents, they fell all over themselves afterward, interrupting each other, describing the fare.

The speeches of Grace Coolidge's husband in Boston were preceded by dinner and followed by drinking and cigar smoke, in which the guest of honor held forth in his nasal voice. At one of them she was so consumed by the unlikelihood of the occasion—her husband the Vermonter who was said to be able to pronounce the word *cow* in four syllables was speaking to these Bostonians—that she hid behind a pillar to conceal her laughter. This address inspired Coolidge to quote several lines by Josiah G. Holland, from the latter's poem "Gradatim," that described what he had done in rising to Massachusetts' political heights, and also brought out his Vermont Yankee pronunciation:

> Heaven is not reached at a single bound;
> But we build the ladder by which we rise
> From the lowly earth to the vaulted skies,
> And we mount to its summit round by round.

That evening Coolidge made the following statement, quoted years later by all his detractors: "The man who builds a factory builds a temple, the man who works there worships there, and to each his due, not scorn and blame, but reverence and praise."

On another occasion, in honor of the hundredth anniversary of the Chickering Piano Company, he outdid himself, evoking surprise as well as mirth from his wife. The house in Northampton had the upright piano in the entranceway, but the man of the house knew absolutely nothing about it nor music of any sort. The visitor saw the nondescript gramophone and no opera records. At the anniversary the orator waxed eloquent on music, composers, and opera. Afterward his wife expressed her amazement at his knowledge, and a smile circled his face and they laughed hilariously. The Chickering Piano Company address was not included in the collected edition of Coolidge addresses, later published.

Such was the life, and the expansion of political activity from Northampton to the statehouse, in which Calvin and Grace Coolidge had their beginning. At the Republican National Convention in Chicago in 1920 there was a small interest in Coolidge for president; he was nominated and his ovation lasted one minute. The convention nominated Senator Warren G. Harding of Ohio. There was talk of the vice presidency, and Murray Crane advised Coolidge's supporters against it: "Don't put the governor up. He's been beaten once and he doesn't want a second defeat." A cabal of senators offered the vice presidential nomination to an also-ran for the presidency, Senator Hiram Johnson of California, who turned it down. The cabal was preparing to nominate Senator Irvine L. Lenroot of Wisconsin, and Lenroot turned it down, when the nomination went to Coolidge. Of all people the instrument was Senator Lodge, who would have been Johnson's running mate for the presidency; he released the Oregon delegation from its pledge to Johnson. The delegates caucused and decided for Coolidge. A leather-lunged former associate justice of the Oregon Supreme Court, Wallace McCamant, stood on a chair and made the nomination:

> When the Oregon delegation came here instructed by the people of our state to present to this convention as its candidate for the office of vice president a distinguished son of Massachusetts [Lodge], he requested that we refrain from mentioning his name. But there is another son of Massachusetts who has been much in the public eye during the past year, a man who is sterling in his Americanism and stands for all that the Republican party holds dear; and on behalf of the Oregon delegation I name for the exalted office of vice president Governor Calvin Coolidge of Massachusetts.

The hall was hot, delegates tired, many had left (banging noises were heard all over the hall as individuals stood up and their trousers stuck to the seats of their collapsible chairs, then the seats banged back down). The convention stampeded for Coolidge.

At a little after eight o'clock that evening, June 12, 1920, Calvin and Grace Coolidge were seated in the Coolidge suite at the Adams House and the telephone rang.[20] As was his wont, the governor picked up the receiver. Putting it down, he turned to his wife. "Nominated for vice president," he said.

Grace Coolidge thought her husband was joking, as he sometimes did, and replied with nonchalance, "You don't mean it."

"Indeed I do," was the response.

"You are not going to accept it, are you?"

Coolidge did not show a shadow of a smile as he answered, "I suppose I shall have to."

The formalities of high national office appeared well before arrival in Washington. After the decision in Chicago, Grace Coolidge wrote a hundred letters and notes to well-wishers.[21] Many more were handled at the statehouse. Then, in the tradition of official notification in American politics, it was necessary to notify the governor of his candidacy on the ticket, and notification had to be in his home territory, Northampton. The family had been to see

Grace experiments in the kitchen with roadway surfacing, c. 1917. Courtesy of the
Forbes Library, Northampton, Massachusetts.

Grandfather Coolidge at the Notch and drove down from there, and as the governor's automobile came into the home city, the decorations were everywhere—bunting on lampposts, draperies of red, white, and blue on buildings, flags on houses. Calvin Jr. in the back seat asked his mother what the display was about, and when she told him it was the notification ceremony for his father, he answered, with boyish reasoning, "Aw, he's known about that for a long time."

Meanwhile, during the campaign and afterward, the two Republican candidates had some political work and then rested from their not very hard labors. The outcome of the campaign was hardly in doubt. Senator Harding for the most part remained on his expanded front porch in Marion and received delegations. Governor Coolidge went to the hinterlands to show the flag. He made a poor speech in Minneapolis and nearly emptied the hall. It did no harm, for the ticket of Harding and Coolidge could not lose. The Democratic candidates, James M. Cox, like Harding from Ohio, and his running mate the young Franklin D. Roosevelt, who had been assistant secretary of the navy in the Wilson administration, could not carry the political baggage of the president. Wilson had insisted on going to the Paris Peace Conference after the World War and taking part in the making of peace. He helped draw up the constitution—the covenant, he described it—of the League of Nations and made it the first twenty-six articles of the Treaty of Versailles with Germany, which the Senate refused to accept. After a speaking tour for the covenant and the treaty, President Wilson on October 2, 1919, suffered a paralytic stroke, and his control over the government in Washington collapsed.

Coolidge went to Kentucky to speak, a state in some danger of going Democratic, and during a time when the Eighteenth Amendment was in effect he made a better impression than in Minnesota. A group of newspapermen invited him to a party and persuaded him to sample the local drink, bourbon. After consuming a glass he was offered a chaser, presumably water, although he must have known it was Kentucky mule. To the surprise of the company he drank it down and failed to change his impassive appearance.

The ticket elected—Harding received a larger percentage of votes than any nominee in American history up to that time—Coolidge and wife performed the last of their duties in Boston, returned to Northampton, and at the invitation of Mr. and Mrs. Stearns went to North Carolina and spent two weeks at Grove Park Inn in Asheville. It was an introduction to the splendors that awaited them. The hotel was up to Washington standards. Near Sunset Mountain looking out on that eminence, it was a row of three- and four-story buildings atop a small rise. The stationery announced the hostelry "absolutely fire-proof," open all year, the "finest resort hotel in the world." On the first day Mrs. Coolidge and Mrs. Stearns each received huge

Calvin and Grace Coolidge, c. 1918.
Courtesy of the Forbes Library, Northampton, Massachusetts.

Governor's first pitch to the Boston Braves.
Courtesy of the Forbes Library, Northampton, Massachusetts.

bouquets of orchids and lilies of the valley, the next day baskets of apples. The Stearnses had been in such places and took them in stride, Mrs. Stearns keeping to her room because of a cold and attacks of sneezing. The Coolidges walked everywhere. Grace Coolidge's husband, after all the concerns of the many years, since the Massachusetts General Assembly in 1907, began to look rested. For the most part the local populace let them alone. The ladies of Asheville gave a reception for Mrs. Coolidge, and 300 people came. The vice president–elect received a reception at the Masonic rooms in the town. All this his wife reported to Therese Hills in Northampton, whom she addressed in letters as "Dearest Pal" and "Pal O'Pals." She signed herself as Susan Ann or Rickety Ann.[22] On February 14 the couple left for New York and a brief return home.

The boys went to Washington for the inauguration and then back to Northampton to finish out the school year, after which they would go—this had not yet been determined—to preparatory school at Mercersburg Academy in Pennsylvania, a hundred miles

Governor and Mrs. Coolidge stand to the left of Frank W. Stearns,
Calvin's foremost friend and booster, and his wife, Emily.
Courtesy of the Forbes Library, Northampton, Massachusetts.

from Washington by circuitous roads, far enough to keep them at
school on weekends and avoid tempting their mother to go up to
see them.

When the Coolidges arrived for the inauguration, they were
greeted at Washington Station by Vice President and Mrs. Thomas
R. Marshall, who like the Stearnses in previous years took them
under their wings. The Marshalls were extraordinarily helpful.
One might not have expected it, for they were not of the same
party and had never seen the Coolidges. The vice president and
wife had not had a pleasant time in Washington during the Wilson
administration, for the president ignored them. Wilson treated his
vice president shabbily; Marshall had not seen the president since
October 1919, when Wilson took ill. He and his wife maintained an
isolated existence in which they carried on their official duties and
said the proper things. To their successors they could not have
been more helpful. They were from North Manchester, Indiana,

which endeared them to residents of Northampton. Best of all, Lois Kinsey Marshall was a Vermonter.

It was the Marshalls who suggested that the Coolidges take over their four-room suite at the Willard. The Willard seemed an acceptable choice, if not the one Grace Coolidge would have made. She would have preferred the Shoreham, where they stayed during a visit to Washington sponsored by Mr. and Mrs. Stearns in 1916, out Connecticut Avenue away from the center of the city; the Willard was on Pennsylvania not far from the White House. But the Willard had advantages. The price was right, eight dollars a day. In a letter to Therese Hills, Grace said she did not need to cook, for she and her husband took meals downstairs in the hotel dining room. She did need to make arrangements for a maid and wrote to the Adams House's Mary, without success. She obtained a nice girl, she said, aged eighteen, to answer the door and telephone, water the plants, and run errands. The girl could mend and sew. She was as sweet and pretty as could be.[23]

An unexpected aspect of the suite at the Willard that Mrs. Coolidge recounted in her autobiography was the mice she met there, a domestic tale worth mentioning, although it is to get ahead of the social entertaining the vice presidency entailed.[24] The mice required entertaining of a different sort. When the Coolidges moved into the hotel, they decided not to use the dining room of the suite and ate in the hotel dining room, and so Grace Coolidge converted the suite dining room into a sitting room by placing a large sofa across a corner. One evening she was sitting there, and a mouse came out from under the sofa. The mouse looked her over and repaired back underneath. Mrs. Coolidge examined the situation and found a round hole along the baseboard above the cement floor. On the first excursion she had given the mouse a few bits of crackers, which he appreciated. He soon brought his family, Mother Gray and several children, and Mrs. Coolidge made it a point to provide the food. She discovered that the young mice liked to climb up the corners of the metal wastebasket and jump into the waste paper, as small boys liked to climb up the beams of a hayloft. After they jumped in, she would tip the wastebasket, and they all scrambled out and did it again. But in August 1923, the Coolidges, who had been in Plymouth Notch, came back to Washington hurriedly and found several rooms added

Grace Coolidge and Emily Stearns (left), who introduced her to the Boston elite.
Courtesy of the Forbes Library, Northampton, Massachusetts.

Neighbors celebrate Coolidge's vice presidential nomination, July 27, 1920.
Courtesy of the Forbes Library, Northampton, Massachusetts.

to the suite, together with stenographers and White House assistants and telephone operators, the Secret Service and reporters outside in the corridor, and she did not know what happened to the family of the Grays.

Housing arranged, Grace Coolidge needed help with the Washington social scene, and Lois Marshall started her off. In her autobiography Mrs. Coolidge likened the situation of her husband and herself to freshmen in a university, who found themselves in strange surroundings. Her husband's case, she believed, was easier than hers, for he was "one of a class of beginners like himself with no particular responsibility to the student body, no conspicuous position to assume, while she must at once become the presiding officer of the advanced class."[25] It was Lois Marshall who introduced her to the group known as the Ladies of the Senate, the largest and most important group she was to meet. The group, which had organized during the war as a unit of the Red Cross and continued as a luncheon club, met every Tuesday in the Senate Office Building when the Senate was in session. Lois Marshall presented her to the ladies on the first full day Mrs. Coolidge was in Washington, March 2, 1921, just before the Democratic administration, the Marshalls with it, went out of office. She named each state the ladies came from. On inauguration day Mrs. Marshall arranged a special tea in the suite at the Willard and introduced the ladies again, so her successor could connect the ninety-six names with the faces.

As wife of the vice president Mrs. Coolidge received on Wednesdays. This was announced in society columns of the papers. The drawing room of the suite at the Willard was not large, and sometimes it was filled. At homes could get out of hand, and during one crowded afternoon a thousand people came for the fare of tea and cakes. A friend drew Mrs. Coolidge aside and told her a bellboy was standing in a corridor on the first floor shouting the directions to the Coolidge suite. The hostess sent word for him to cease and desist, lest she entertain everyone on Pennsylvania Avenue.

Calling on wives of officials was not as hard on her as for others, but she had to call on wives of Supreme Court justices, cabinet officers, and heads of diplomatic missions. This took an afternoon each week. Quarries not at home, she left cards.

Out-of-town visitors swarmed in to see their friends the Coolidges. The inauguration brought the first wave, and thereafter more rolled in, mostly from Massachusetts, Northampton of course, or Boston. One day her husband's former law partner's relatives came.

The rush of appointments or engagements was without end, and there was not much Grace Coolidge could do about it other than meet it. She wrote Therese Hills plaintively that she could hardly remember the afternoons the two spent together in Northampton, with nothing to do other than talk and darn socks.[26] On a typical day in Washington she went to a luncheon, saw a woman at the hotel apartment at 3:00, went to a reception at 4:30, and from there to a concert by the Philadelphia Orchestra. The Coolidges ate out almost every evening (her husband supposedly explained, "Gotta eat somewhere"). "I had no conception of the actual demands upon my time," his wife wrote. "It is one mad rush." She engaged a secretary, two hours three times a week, and that helped. She and her husband sought to save Thursday nights so they could be alone. Her husband set deadlines for entertainments, after which they had to leave. For teas his deadline for Grace was six o'clock. For dinners it was ten, whereupon he might say something like, "Grace, we're leaving." When she was not present he would call and say, "Grace, I've come home. You come home, too."[27]

In Burlington, Grace's father and mother subscribed to the *Washington Post* and after reading the social columns for a couple of weeks decided the capital was no place for them to see their daughter. They determined to meet her in Northampton, whenever she was there.[28]

In such manner the Coolidges carried on, from March 1921 until August 1923.

Politically speaking their presence in Washington was insecure, although they had no idea of how much so. President Harding graciously asked his vice president to attend cabinet meetings; Coolidge was the first vice president to do so. The vice president knew a gesture when he saw one, and said little. The assistant secretary of the navy, Theodore Roosevelt Jr., who attended the meetings in absence of the secretary, never heard Coolidge offer an opinion on a major question.[29] The president otherwise gave Coolidge no attention. Grace Coolidge complained to her friend Therese Hills that her husband found it difficult to run an office with a single secretary and one stenographer when as governor he had two secretaries and several stenographers, not to mention other help.[30] Harding described Coolidge as "the little fellow" to the Republican leader of the Senate, Charles Curtis of Kansas, who became vice president in the Herbert Hoover administration. He told Curtis he was going to arrange for the director of the budget, Brigadier General Charles G. Dawes, to be his running mate, to succeed him.[31] The president's opinion of the vice president appeared in the behavior of his plain-speaking wife when in 1922 the widow of a senator from Missouri, Mrs. John B. Henderson, offered her large house on Fourteenth Street, known as Henderson Castle, as a vice presidential residence. A bill had been introduced in Congress to accept the offer. According to the president of Columbia University, Nicholas Murray Butler, who with Mrs. Butler was visiting at the White House and telling Florence Harding of the suitability of the castle, the president's wife became increasingly impatient and finally burst out shouting, "Not a bit of it, not a bit of it. I am going to have that bill defeated. Do you think

I am going to have those Coolidges living in a house like that? An hotel apartment is plenty good enough for them."[32]

One thing the Coolidges were aware of was their largely unknown existence among the citizens of the capital who had little or nothing to do with the Coolidges' entertaining in Washington. The vice president and his wife seem to have considered their relative anonymity as quaint, of minor importance, in any event something they could do little about. A story made the rounds of a fire at the Willard, during which everyone came down to the first floor, where they milled around in various states of dress. When everything seemed over, Vice President Coolidge started up the stairs to his suite. The fire marshal halted him. "Who are you?" asked that functionary.

"I'm the vice president," Coolidge replied.

"All right—go ahead," said the marshal.

Coolidge went a step or two and was halted a second time. "What are you vice president of?" the marshal asked suspiciously.

"I'm the vice president of the United States."

"Come right down," said the marshal. "I thought you were the vice president of the hotel."

Anonymity was symbolized by the addition of a middle initial on a complimentary pass issued by the National Baseball League, which designated him Calvin G. Coolidge. The American League gave him a pass for Calvin C. Coolidge.[33]

One day his wife was late leaving the Willard for Continental Hall and forgot her ticket. She said to the doorman that she was Mrs. Coolidge.[34]

The doorman looked at her. "What's your husband's first name?"

"Calvin."

"What's his business?"

"He's vice president."

"Vice president of what?"

In 1923 there was some evidence that President Harding was in poor health. That summer a Boston friend was talking to the Coolidges in their suite and told them Harding was in failing health and that Coolidge would be president. To this the then vice president said nothing. Mrs. Coolidge was playing solitaire on the back of the piano and remarked, "What a thing to say!" In the last days of July, Coolidge's secretary in Washington, Edward T. Clark, was sending messages to Plymouth Notch, where the Coolidges were visiting the vice president's father, that the ill president in San Francisco was worse off than newspaper reports revealed.[35] These were signs, and Coolidge's predecessor Marshall had heard the same talk about President Wilson.

Then, suddenly, the Coolidges found themselves at the center of national attention.

CHAPTER 3

"SHE TOOK PRECEDENCE OVER ME": THE NEW FIRST LADY

In her autobiography, Grace Coolidge wrote about her appearance in the White House: "There was a sense of detachment—this was I and yet not I, this was the wife of the President of the United States and she took precedence over me; my personal likes and dislikes must be subordinated to the consideration of those things which were required of her."[1] The White House, 1600 Pennsylvania Avenue, traffic moving on the street, people walking along the iron fence, casting glances at the magnificent eighteenth-century building with the white columns, the walkway on the west leading to the presidential offices erected during the Theodore Roosevelt administration—the building burned in 1929, replaced by another containing the Oval Office—and on the east a colonnade passing to the less prestigious (in 1923–1929 not yet built) East Wing. This was no larger version of the Willard apartment, and Mrs. Coolidge felt a sense of awe as she came in the front entrance on August 21, after Florence Harding returned from Marion, Ohio, and the entombment of her husband and moved out to a friend's house before returning to the city of her birth. That first afternoon when President and Mrs. Coolidge arrived it was warm but not sweltering, windows open, breeze blowing, flowers filling the rooms, all awaiting their arrival as if they had returned from a luncheon or early afternoon tea.

Grace Coolidge knew without hesitation the names of the first ladies beginning with Edith Roosevelt; she had been in college in 1901 when the assassin fired the bullet in Buffalo and William McKinley lingered a few days and died. She could recite stories of their personalities, as well as those of their husbands. This, to be sure, was her immediate inspiration as first lady. The term went back to 1849 when President Zachary Taylor announced the death of Dolley Madison and so described her. From the presidency's beginning in 1789 it was possible to see two sorts of presidential wives: those who, like Martha Washington, considered their task ceremonial in support of their husbands, and those who followed the precepts of the wife of John Adams, the inimitable Abigail, who advised their husbands and anyone else, ready or not. But in the early years few of the first ladies stood out in public view, whatever their qualities, because until the very late nineteenth century newspapers could not reproduce photographs (they used artists and woodcuts, five times as expensive and much slower in preparation); public interest hence was not there. Beginning in 1901 everything was different, what with photogravures, rotogravures, and other print changes, and the first lady tradition developed with startling suddenness.

Mrs. Coolidge put her stamp on the tradition in several ways. One was to bring in a first-rate social secretary, who assisted the predecessor secretary. She dismissed the housekeeper and defended the action against that harridan's smart-alecky book, *Secrets of the White House,* slapped together and published the next year.[2] She sought to replace the miscellany of furniture on the second floor where her family lived and in some of the public rooms, producing an uproar from architects and self-appointed experts who believed they knew better. When the mansion's roof had to be replaced in 1927, opportunity arose for modest household changes, which she quietly made.

Her principal contribution as first lady was twofold, one inadvertent, the other virtually that, both securing her reputation as the great lady she was.

In development of the institution of first lady after the McKinley administration, the first presidential wives, Edith Roosevelt and Helen Taft, were markedly different, and the results for their husbands admirable and deplorable as the one husband expected, the other might have.[3] Theodore Roosevelt needed no boost from his wife, but she helped in large ways. When he was governor, she stood beside him in his first reception in Albany, and being a New York socialite and perhaps therefore not enjoying the old-time American habit of shaking hands, she arranged to carry a bouquet of flowers, with both hands, and smiled as the hand shakers sought to tackle her ebullient husband. In the White House she engaged a skilled social secretary, Isabelle Hagner, although at first brought her in to manage the White House debut of her husband's daughter (born of his first wife, who died in childbirth). The impetuous daughter could not be asked to assist with her own coming out. Task accomplished in January 1902, Edith accomplished another. The mansion's mistress managed renovation of the White House by Charles F. McKim of the New York firm of McKim, Mead and White. The Roosevelt family let McKim clear out the Victorian bric-a-brac including a Louis Tiffany screen in the front reception room, and create a French Empire decor that it never had possessed; whatever, it was far better than the eclecticism that prevailed and possessed the special virtue of creation of the West Wing, housing the presidential offices, ridding the living quarters upstairs of the offices that had crowded presidential families into unconscionably close quarters. The West Wing also allowed McKim to get rid of the clutch of ugly greenhouses attached to the mansion, which the architect rightly believed detracted from its lines. All this done, Edith arranged for a White House china collection displayed on the ground floor and a White House first ladies portrait gallery, distinctly lesser achievements.

Compared with Edith Roosevelt's accomplishments, the presence of her successor, Helen Taft, admittedly for only four years, did not achieve nearly as much. Mrs. Taft ardently desired to be first lady and pushed her corpulent, sedentary husband away from offers of a Supreme Court appointment, which he would have loved, into an office for which he did not fit, as he did not enjoy politics at all. She rode back with him in the inaugural carriage, a novelty not followed by her immediate successors. Having enjoyed being in the Philippines at the governor general's palace, the Malacañang, full of servants, she hired and outfitted a group of doormen and outfitted them in livery, which seemed a little much for the building sometimes known by its original name, the People's House. She suffered a stroke two months into her husband's term and although managing a slow recovery could not thereafter be fully active. She followed Edith Roosevelt's innovation of musicales and attempted lawn parties with modest success (when one of them was rained out after the weatherman predicted sunshine, she talked, perhaps not seriously, of shooting the weatherman). The result of her ambitious presence, apart from her husband's defeat for reelection in 1912 (she may have borne a considerable responsibility by pushing him into an office he could not easily fill), was her arrangement to obtain Japanese cherry trees to surround the Potomac basin, visible ever since to residents and visitors.

The first Mrs. Wilson, the fragile Ellen, who died of Bright's disease in August 1914, took one measure to exert her personality, worthy in itself but of little result save to encourage photographers to display, easy to do, the appalling shanties of African American residents so close to the Capitol building that they stood in the same photograph, the dome looming over the shacks as if it represented another world, which it did. She sought better living quarters for these fellow citizens, an enterprise her racist husband accepted, perhaps because it removed attention from his own backward policies. For the rest of it she advocated amateur painting, of which she was almost a professional. Her strength ran out, and she passed on.

President Wilson remarried a bare year after Ellen Wilson's death, to the widow of a Washington jeweler, and her effect from 1915 to 1921 was, in the estimation of some historians, present writer included, nothing less than deplorable, considering the care and for the most part small initiatives of her three twentieth-century predecessors. The full effect of President Wilson's second marriage to this conniving yet simpleminded woman probably can never be measured. The present pages certainly are an improper place for any approximate attempt. She did not leave any heritage of lasting changes in the institution of the first lady, for her marriage came when the European war was stalemating, and a year and few months later the United States entered the war, making it a world war. White House social events ceased. Where the conniving entered was her efforts to undermine the president's close adviser, Edward M. House, a Texas colonel whom she described privately as Colonel Mouse; at the Paris peace conference House's authority diminished to insignificance.

Meanwhile, she sought a transfer of her husband's private secretary, Joseph P. Tumulty, a domestic political figure both loyal and politically sensitive, having come from the byzantine politics of the state of New Jersey. After her husband and she (she accompanied him) returned from the peace conference and made a swing around the country in support of the League of Nations, he suffered the paralytic stroke and was a hopeless invalid from that time through the remaining months of the presidency and until his death in 1924. Until February 1920, over three months, she refused to reveal the nature of his illness, until the president's distinguished urologist, Hugh Young of Johns Hopkins, frankly revealed it to a reporter, wishing no part in a plot of silence. Even then, for the remainder of the presidency, Mrs. Wilson undertook to receive and take in to the sick room what messages, and in a form she chose, she believed her husband could see. The simplemindedness came from her footloose description: "I myself never made a single decision regarding the disposition of public affairs. . . . The only decision that was made was what was important and what was not, and the very important decision of when to present matters to my husband."[4]

As mentioned, her evaluation may never be possible. She called in a skilled professional writer and historian to handle her memoirs, published after the Coolidges were out of the White House, in 1939. Marquis James wrote what she told him and toned down her vitriolic remarks in papers now in the Library of Congress, such as a description of Senator Lodge as a snake.[5] She died long after her era, in 1961. There is no evidence, incidentally, that the public record of her White House experiences influenced Grace Coolidge or produced even private remarks by her observant husband; the tempestuous reign of Edith Wilson, if such it was, apparently had no effect upon them.

Preceding Grace Coolidge was of course Florence Harding, whose years as first lady, at least their public record, were placid compared with those of her immediate predecessor. Mrs. Harding received a careful press, respectful of the fact that she was five years older than her husband, born in 1860, and did not carry her years well. She suffered bouts of kidney disease, from which she was near death during an attack in September–December 1922. She dressed with care and expensively, with elaborate gowns that covered her swollen legs; she often wore a choker necklace to cover the wrinkles of her throat. She spoke occasionally to reporters, glad to be quoted, and made remarks from the White House south portico in a high-pitched, critics said rasping, voice. She referred to her husband as "Warren Harding," which seemed odd. She and her friends patronized a local fortune-teller, a harmless enjoyment, speculated upon. Florence Harding's two large accomplishments as first lady were to throw open the White House grounds to the public, veritably to open what during the illness of President Wilson had seemed a gated, fenced-off mansion. She made a special and most attractive personal project of visiting the world war patients in Walter Reed Hospital, blinded or gassed or with missing legs and arms. To them she brought bunches of flowers, individually tied from the White House greenhouses by that time on the south side of the mall. She and her husband invited hundreds of them, in wheelchairs and ambulatory, to White House garden parties, all with a receiving line and food, and music furnished by the red-uniformed Marine Band.

Talk of scandal arose during the administration, none of it large or touching the president. After Harding's death his widow soon died, of a heart attack similar to that of her husband, and a bewildering series of assertions of foul play arose, not a single one credible. A high school student whom Harding, then a senator, sought to befriend accused him of adultery with her daughter as proof. From all available evidence Nanna P. Britton was a liar. Years later existence of a liaison with the wife of a neighbor in Marion, Carrie Phillips, revealed a ten-year affair, from 1905 to 1915. Letters showed Mrs. Phillips attempting blackmail of the presidential candidate, of a serious sort that Florence Harding had to know about because it threatened their financial solvency; her husband's lawyer settled it satisfactorily. Florence Harding, an understanding wife, stood by her husband in this mess, somewhat akin to the affairs of Grover Cleveland and Alexander Hamilton, not to mention Benjamin Franklin. The simplicity of what happened in the Britton and Phillips accusations brought out the American nation's love of scandal, duly catered to by one convicted felon who accused Florence Harding, suitably in 1930 when death had silenced her, of murdering her husband, an impossibility in San Francisco in 1923 when he was surrounded by five physicians.[6]

John, Grace, the president, and Colonel John.
Courtesy of the Forbes Library, Northampton, Massachusetts.

In regard to the White House, the mansion, and supervising its personnel, Grace Coolidge made two changes, the first an easy appointment, bringing in her part-time social secretary during the vice presidency, Mary Randolph, as assistant to Florence Harding's secretary Laura Harlan, daughter of Supreme Court justice John M. Harlan. Miss Randolph came in December 1923, when the social season made her presence, or that of someone with similar talents, necessary. Laura Harlan resigned in March 1925, her place filled by Mary Randolph.[7]

A small, thin individual, with an office in an alcove behind the window of the front portico where she could see everyone who came in the front door, Mary Randolph possessed three telephones and saw a daily rush of seekers of appointments with or favors from the first lady. She was the soul of efficiency and gave time unstintingly to avalanches, she wrote in her admirable memoir, of telephone calls, letters, notes, appeals, demands, appointments, and errands, here, there, and everywhere, in all parts of the building, and when she went home, the work often followed her.

Miss Randolph grew up in Washington and fondly remembered the debut of Alice Roosevelt when at a tumultuous moment the president's daughter jumped on a sofa in the East Room, collecting the attention of everyone, and then jumped to the floor in honor of some wild instinct. The two were contemporaries. She knew social usage and local socialites without having to consult a book. She accompanied Mrs. Coolidge to many of the latter's appointments; the two got along well, and the first lady gladly let Miss Randolph handle the details of everything that found its way into her frantic alcove. Miss Randolph's sole objection to her position with Grace Coolidge (she remained until near the end of the succeeding Hoover administration) was her salary, around $3,000, which she believed should be raised. By act of Congress, not the act of the husband of her employer, who wanted to raise her $60 a year, it went up to $3,200, which, living as a single woman in an apartment, she found manageable. At home she enjoyed the assistance of a maid.

The other personnel change in the mansion under Grace Coolidge was the dismissal of the housekeeper, Elizabeth Jaffray, whose departure was nominally in all friendliness but in fact was not. Helen Taft had brought Mrs. Jaffray in after Edith Roosevelt ridded herself of the McKinleys' housekeeper, because the wife of the Republican Roosevelt desired to manage the White House staff herself. Mrs. Jaffray, arriving in 1909, enjoyed a suite on the White House's second floor, probably a nuisance to the Coolidges. But her basic problem was her residence in the mansion too long. She controlled eighteen domestic servants, including kitchen help, excluding the first lady's maid and the president's valet. She acted toward the Coolidges as if she held special rights to her duties and considered White House occupants temporary people who came and went. There was truth to this point, but the housekeeper had no need to dispense it in her *Secrets of the White House.* She wrote in detail of the Coolidges' niggardly ways. Mrs. Coolidge was not amused and in one of the robin letters spoke out against her with unaccustomed sharpness.[8] The book came out first in a series of articles in *Cosmopolitan*, and she knew some of the robins had been reading them. She told the robins what the White House butler who had been in the mansion for ten years told Mrs. Stearns after the first article: "It's too bad some of us can't write what we know about her." Grace

Two friends. Courtesy of the Forbes Library, Northampton, Massachusetts.

Coolidge said it was a pity that the housekeeper could not have written something interesting when she broke into print. "I particularly regretted the article on the Hardings but any intelligent person must have seen that the author was queer and not to be taken seriously." Mrs. Jaffray wrote that when Mrs. Harding went to the White House to look over the mansion prior to her husband's presidency, she affronted the sensibilities of Mrs. Wilson, evident in the latter's sending for Mrs. Jaffray to take the about-to-be first lady over the house. Instead the two presidential wives had gotten on well, with protestations of friendship, and it was in fact tactful to send for the housekeeper. The latter wrote of the Coolidges that she had been ashamed to use a horse and carriage to go to market in the capital; Mrs. Coolidge said that with no intention of humiliation it happened that a horse instead of an automobile was the only means placed at her disposal. Mrs. Jaffray told how much President Coolidge was saving from his salary; that, said the wife of her employer, was ridiculous, for she could not have known. Mrs. Coolidge said the reason the Coolidge family seemed so strange to Mrs. Jaffray was that the Coolidges were rather normal and did not appreciate her. On July 1, 1926, Ellen A. Riley came to take Mrs. Jaffray's place, and everything thereafter was peaceful. She had managed the R. H. Stearns Department Store cafeteria and before that, during the war, the food service at one of the army's cantonment camps.

Mrs. Jaffray spread stories about how the Coolidges skimped on food for White House dinners so they could take the money home to Northampton. Another spreader of stories was the White House head usher, Irwin H. (Ike) Hoover, who after retiring at the beginning of the Franklin Roosevelt administration published a tell-all book that, like Mrs. Jaffray's, was put together from scrappy if much more voluminous material and excoriated Coolidge for being tight with everything. He repeated Mrs. Jaffray's canard of how at night Coolidge prowled the White House kitchen to count the hams on the serving tables. This had its origin in Hoover's irritation, communicated to Dr. Boone, that President Coolidge would not raise his salary, with the result that Hoover's assistant because of receiving veterans' preference, a supplement for veterans administered by the Veterans' Bureau, had a higher salary than his senior. Coolidge himself told the ham story, after retirement, in half humor, to a writer, James C. Derieux. "Those White House hams," he said. "They worried me most of all. A big one would be brought to the table. Mrs. Coolidge would have a slice, and I'd have one. The butler would take it away, and what happened to it after that I never could find out."[9] What happened probably was something the Coolidges had not known in New England, which was the habit in kitchens in the South of giving "totin' privileges" to workers therein.

As for changes in the White House itself, apart from personnel, Grace Coolidge found the task so formidable—unlike her predecessor Edith Roosevelt who in the McKim restoration moved with little or no hesitation and total success in getting changes she wanted—that she discovered herself almost hemmed in and accomplished little. Years before, the unappreciative President Chester A. Arthur had sold original pieces of White House furniture in favor of Victorian furniture. McKim's decor for the White House, including the furnishings, had been Empire, alien to the structure that was an enlarged Federal-style building, nothing Napoleonic about it. The first lady knew well how McKim had thrown out precious chandeliers, one of them gold, in favor of his style; members of Congress, presumably Democrats she wrote privately to a friend, had rescued them from the White House scrap heap and positioned them around the Capitol building. In 1925 a congressional appropriation of $50,000 seemed to give opportunity to make a change in furniture. Congress thoughtfully stipulated where most of the money would go. It was to fix the dilapidated elevator from the first to second floor, replace wallpaper in the Green Room where the sun had faded it to a jaded brown, modernize the vacuum system, replace rugs, and do minor upholstering of furniture. Mrs. Coolidge espied an opportunity and sought to seize it. She sensed opportunity to obtain antique American colonial furniture by private donation—the 1920s marked the height of the antique craze in America, and her idea was to install the best of colonial furniture by solicitation, for being from New England she knew it was out there in private hands. She would have labeled it with names of donors. But the initial attempt to secure private gifts of furniture, tentatively proposed in April 1925, brought no gifts and the vociferous objection of the American Institute of Architects that summer, which sent a letter to the president. There was talk of enlisting the widow of President Roosevelt, and Mrs. Frances Folsom Preston, widow of President Cleveland.

To do anything about the White House after McKim had his way was deemed utterly wrong, and no innocent presentation of the idea permissible. Grace Coolidge tried again, August 28, 1926, when the wife of the publisher of the *Saturday Evening Post,* Mrs. George Horace Lorimer, no small personality, quite evidently after talking with the first lady, announced that Mrs. Coolidge was about to make a public appeal for the best of American colonial furniture, by Chippendale, Heppelwhite, Sheraton, and Phyfe. Two days later the first lady's cautious husband squelched the proposal before she could make it. In his press conference, where he forced reporters to attribute anything he said to "the White House spokesman," so if necessary he could deny it, he told the newspaper press that such a proposal was impossible, that while the first lady was the mansion's "next friend," the idea could not fly. On this score Mrs. Coolidge was helpless.[10]

The next year, 1927, the White House roof had to be replaced, the Coolidges moving out of the mansion for 127 days to a mansion on Dupont Circle owned by the daughter of Mrs. Robert M. Patterson, owner of the *Chicago Tribune*. The daughter was the former "Cissie" Patterson, who became the Countess Gizycka before she married Elmer Schlesinger and moved to New York. An opportunity opened for the first lady to make physical changes in the White House attic and in some of the second-floor rooms ignored by McKim. Mrs. Coolidge made them, with little public notice. Congress appropriated $375,000 for the roof, which involved removing everything from the attic and labeling it. Walls of the second floor were covered with muslin to protect them from dust, the same with the first floor. With a temporary roof overhead, huge derricks and covered chutes took down the roof and attic beams. Steel beams replaced the split wooden beams held up by posts. As work went on, the White House seemed almost the same but in fact the architect, a relative of Franklin Roosevelt, William Adams Delano, redesigned the whole attic, allowing new guest and servant rooms with baths. He installed closets in the house; prior to that time storage of clothes, sheets, pillowcases, and so on was in freestanding closets, the usual arrangement for eighteenth- and nineteenth-century houses.[11]

Atop the mansion to the rear, extending from the roof, was a novelty that Grace Coolidge found delightful, which she enjoyed for her last year and a half in the White House. She described it as a sky parlor, and everyone understood that when she was there she was not to be disturbed. This retreat contained a cot, a writing table, porch furniture, a Victrola, and a portable radio. The room had glass and Venetian blinds on three sides. She was there with friends on the day the *Graf Zeppelin* passed overhead. On the table stood the radio, "with no connection with the outside world," bringing music from a station far away, and up there floated "that huge man-made conveyance" that had crossed the ocean. She pinched herself, she wrote, to make certain she was awake and not dreaming of a world unborn.[12]

The only trouble with the Coolidge roof was the near-total ignorance of Delano, who was far more of a decorator than an architect, and his co-expert, an army officer, U. S. Grant III, whose nominal authority was director of the capital's parks and grounds. Delano and Grant put 180 tons of cement ("a clumsy lid") on top of the masonry shell of the old building and the bearing walls within. This forced the complete tearing down of the White House twenty years later by Coolidge's successor Harry S. Truman, who with his family moved across the street to the Blair-Lee House and remained there until 1952, during which the old house was gutted to the walls and rebuilt from scratch—making the present-day White House a reproduction of what the Coolidges knew.[13]

The first of Grace Coolidge's two principal contributions to her special position of wife of the president of the United States was her reputation of being among the best-dressed women of her time, virtually the leader of fashion during her husband's presidential years. None of her predecessors including Edith Roosevelt caught press attention in this way—every gown or other accoutrement of dress, formal or informal, brought her onto the fashion pages of newspapers. By and large, let it be added, apart from the publicity she never gave evidence of cultivating, for it would have been against her heritage from Burlington with which she lived throughout her long life, but which she undoubtedly knew was a credit both to herself and to her presidential husband, she was a leader in good taste among well-dressed women of the 1920s when, emerging from the dowdyism of earlier years, women "came out," to use the popular phrase. When fashions threatened to become extreme in the liberating decade, she held them in check.

Her ability as a fashion leader started when she was growing up and her mother made her clothes and Lemira Goodhue taught her to be a seamstress. When at Clarke, she made her own clothes and continued to do so through the Northampton years when money was short, until the lieutenant governorship, governorship, and into the vice presidency, in the latter two offices of which her husband earned $10,000 a year and she had no time for homemade clothes. She told Boone that she liked to make alterations in her dresses, even repairs, although she had a maid who was available for such things. By the time of the presidency she was too busy for that, and store alterations took over.[14]

Calvin Coolidge's desire for his wife to look her best started with hats. When she was still in Northampton, she met her husband in Springfield and they went window-shopping, where he saw a woman's hat for sale that he liked—a picture hat, with a wide brim and a rose, and he bought it on the spot. When she returned and went into his law office, the secretary and her assistant told her how much they liked the new hat, and her eyes sparkled as she told how she obtained it. She had gone into the store certain that the hat would cost too much. With the hat on her head she inquired, "How much is it?"

The answer was, "Nineteen dollars and ninety-eight cents."

To her surprise her husband said, "We'll take it and she will wear it."

He gave the clerk a twenty-dollar bill, from which his change was two cents. As they walked down the street he would look at her slyly and then at the pennies he had in hand. He said not a single word about the cost.[15]

Another hat story was of how she came into the living room at 21 Massasoit Street one day and saw her husband sitting in the Morris chair holding one of her hats between his legs, with the crown up, measuring it with a piece of string. She said nothing and watched while he carefully tied a small knot where the circled string came around to its starting point. He wound the string around two fingers and slipped it off and put it in a notebook he always carried. Later, when the family was going up to the Notch to see his father, Mrs. Coolidge noticed a large hat box on top of her husband's luggage. They went by train to Ludlow from whence they drove the twelve miles to his father's house. After the greetings of arrival he opened the box and uncovered a large leghorn hat laced with dark blue taffeta silk. A pink rose was artistically arranged on the brim. She thereupon knew what the string had been for. That summer she could not go out of the Notch house without wearing the hat. "I have no doubt," she testified, "the neighbors thought I was 'high-hatting' them."[16]

Hats, the biographer Ross reported, cost between eighteen and sixty dollars. The president liked the large picture hats with roses, and generally the more of the latter the better. She had to win him over to the cloches, helmets, and turbans of the 1920s.[17]

But it was in dresses that Grace Coolidge obtained a national reputation as a fashion leader. Here the president desired her to spend whatever the dress and occasion demanded, and word got out, with no comment from the White House or its spokesman, that the dress bill one day from a large Washington shop was $1,000, dresses averaging $200. In the currency of eighty years later the day's outlay was $11,710, dresses at $2,340.[18]

Without exception each dress set the fashion world agog and received full press coverage. The first lady shopped for some herself, perhaps in the company of Mary Randolph, whom she often consulted. Some dresses came on approval after her husband in the company of his Secret Service guard, Colonel Edmund W. Starling, window-shopped early upon walking down Washington streets. At the outset of the presidency Miss Randolph remembered purchases of a dark blue gabardine street dress, "with long side panels floating free of the skirt, embroidered in coral silk; a fur coat of tan-colored caracal." Another one, much handsomer, was of sealskin. The social secretary saw an ermine evening wrap and a gold brocade evening gown with Persian colors woven through it, bands of rubies and brilliants over the shoulders.

There were gorgeous lamés with long court trains of gold lace—a *robe de style* of bright pink taffeta, the skirt bordered by a deep flounce of silver lace, and with a spray of silk flowers appliquéd across the front. For the morning, she was fond of simple knitted dresses, which were very becoming to her trim figure, and she had them in several colors.[19]

At the diplomatic reception, December 15, 1923,

Mrs. Coolidge did, indeed, look like a youthful, dignified bride in her gown of heavy white satin brocaded in medium-sized figures in white. The gown was made in waistlineless style, slightly draped, but not enough to interfere with the straight effect. It had shoulder straps about an inch wide, of the same material as the gown, with a long, square-cut court train of the material hanging from the low décolleté in the back and trailing at least three feet. Without doubt, one of the reasons this gown was "so very good looking," as all the women present pronounced it, was because it was absolutely devoid of trimming of any kind, the richness of the material being enough embellishment.[20]

The society columnist of the *Washington Post*, whose sobriquet was "Dolly Madison," on February 8, 1925, vowed that Mrs. Coolidge was stunning at the congressional reception the night before. "Mrs. Coolidge looked so well: she wore a gown of gold lace over gold tissue and edged with bands of gold tissue. It was tremendously becoming—and gold always seems to me to be becoming to very few."

Her street wear was equally attractive. Without being extreme in 1926–1929, avoiding the very short skirts of the time when ugly knees stood out as if they were wooden, she wore

> smart coat suits and sport coats, each worn with just exactly the proper style of hat and other accessories. A rose color hat with a rather wider brim than that of her sport hats is worn with a gray tailored coat and at the speedboat races here a week ago her sports costume portrayed the latest effect in garments of that kind. The skirt (and every woman is watching assiduously to see if she is adding an inch to the length of either coat or skirt) was of heavy white crepe, a little longer than those worn by ultra-fashionable women, and was plaited at the front. The blouse was of heavy red silk and wool crepe, showing a plait in the back for fullness and buttoned to the throat in front. She wore a soft white felt hat becomingly curved at the brim. For the opening of a new theatre this week she wore an emerald green gown of chiffon, and over it a coat of soft white satin with a white fur collar.[21]

At a wedding early in November 1927 she appeared almost entirely in red.

> The gown of claret red satin showed several ultra features, such as a cluster of close shirrings at the lower edge of the blouse, which was cut in surplice effect, and just below it another cluster of shirrings, which gave a full effect to the front of the skirt. A rose plaiting several inches deep around the hemline of the skirt at the front, and the tightly fitted sleeves showed draped cuffs. Her hat was red and wide of brim, and her shoes, showing several straps, were of black satin. A handsome black fox and a beaded bag mounted in silver finished her costume.[22]

The other, more important, contribution of Grace Coolidge's years as first lady was the sheer charm she exerted, effortless as it seemed with anyone she met. The charm by no means resulted from her being at peace with herself, for she was deeply emotional and her mind often moved in tumultuous ways. But she knew what she represented, obtained from Burlington before she met her husband, and charmed everyone with the clear-eyed simplicity of those formative years.

Charm was her principal legacy to the first lady tradition. As in her leadership in women's fashion she did not choose it as her legacy to the institution in which she found herself. Her husband forbade any public action that looked in the direction of, not to mention touched upon, politics. If she had wished to take leadership in any public cause, as did Ellen Wilson for the poor in Washington, or Florence Harding with women's rights (Mrs. Harding had been a businesswoman in Marion, running the finances of her husband's newspaper, the *Marion Star*), her husband in his Victorian way would not have allowed it. One time she saw two prominent women from one of the largest states privately in the White House who had something or other they wished to discuss. At lunch that day she told her husband about it. He inquired what their session was, and she said it was political interest. "He said with quite a little irritation, 'Did you tell them you didn't know anything about politics?'" Mrs. Coolidge replied quickly, "They found that out in one minute, if not in two minutes." Frances Parkinson Keyes, wife of Senator Henry Keyes of New Hampshire, a prominent novelist and also a commentator on politics in the 1920s, enjoyed a cordial relationship with Grace Coolidge during the Coolidge vice presidency but found herself dropped from nearly all contact with her friend when the latter became first lady; insensitive to Grace's need to drop her, she wrote querulously about it, never understanding why her former friend had excluded her from intimacy.[23]

Charm, it was true, was the only nonpolitical action left for the first lady—other than sponsorship of an endowment for the Clarke School in 1928–1929, which was safe enough because the initiative was that of a financial journalist in New York, Clarence W. Barron, who lined up large contributors and died the year he advanced the enterprise (see chapter 5).

Her prohibition from politics nonetheless bore an advantage. It allayed the fears of men about first ladies, fears aroused by Helen Taft, the second Mrs. Wilson, and Florence Harding. When the Nineteenth Amendment became law, with women voting for the

The first lady visits in 1924 the Clarke School for the Deaf,
where she both taught and served as a trustee.
Courtesy of the Forbes Library, Northampton, Massachusetts.

first time in national elections (they had voted in state elections, and one state, Montana, sent a woman to the House of Representatives, Jeannette Rankin, who made herself prominent, too prominent many men said, by voting against the declaration of war in 1917), there was fear of a "women's vote." A near generation earlier Theodore Roosevelt's daughter Alice, the "princess," as she was described, had been not merely socially prominent but frequently, men allowed, unconventional. Grace Coolidge did not threaten men. Her careful staying behind her husband—in public events her husband actually walked ahead of her—sat well with the men of the country.

Mrs. Coolidge championed women but did not do it obtrusively. On April 18, 1925, she pushed a button inaugurating the Woman's World Fair in Chicago, which celebrated the commercial achievements of women. At the Columbian Exposition of 1893 in Chicago, only one occupation of women was celebrated, needlework; now there were seventy, among them invention, commerce, art, banking, oil drilling, and steer raising. On Mother's Day that year she represented the Gold Star Mothers at the Tomb of the Unknown Soldier in Arlington. The year before she awarded prizes for the War Department in an essay contest open to girls and young women who wrote of why young men they knew should attend the citizens' military training camps conducted by the department each summer, to which her two sons had gone.[24] She inaugurated her 1928–1929 social season by entertaining at a tea the women writers of Washington.[25]

As mentioned, she charmed everyone she met. Even the perplexed Mrs. Keyes, who could be vitriolic in her economic security as a popular writer, together with her husband's safe Senate seat, wrote, "She is the one woman in official life of whom I have never heard a single disparaging remark in the course of nearly twenty years."[26]

Similarly she charmed children, which everyone noticed. When they called upon her at the White House to present flowers or perhaps Girl Scout cookies, she shook hands with them, the photographers always in evidence—although she would have done it without photographers. One youngster saw in a newspaper the blind and deaf Helen Keller hugging her (and the one thinks embarrassed president too) and told his mother he would like to meet Mrs. Coolidge and have her hug him; she duly obliged, afterward telling a friend she believed she might become known as the National Hugger.[27] At one of the White House egg-rolling festivals, held annually on the south grounds of the mansion, she met a nine-year-old towheaded youngster, Robert Merrill, and his older sister Christine, aged thirteen, and gave him a mouth organ, his sister a doll complete with shoes. At the next festival she encountered him, greeted him, talked with him as she went along amid the 30,000 other boys and girls and chaperones. "What did Mrs. Coolidge say?" Robert was asked by his playmates. "She said she remembered me. Asked me what I could play on my mouth organ," he explained. "And she wanted to know how Christine was and if I saw the raccoon she had with her in the morning."[28] (Rebecca Raccoon was a household pet of both Coolidges, who draped her around their necks, until Rebecca tried once too often to escape captivity and had to be sent to the Washington Zoo.)

Vera Bloom, the bright and witty daughter of Congressman Sol Bloom from New York City, who wrote one of the most delightful memoirs of her years in Washington, measured Grace Coolidge and although from a solidly Democratic family found her wonderful. "Her grace and charm," she said at the conference on world welfare of the Women's Universal Alliance, May 6, 1927, "are real assets to the White House, and contribute much to the prestige of the administration." Then in the vernacular of New York she underlined the point: "Mrs. Coolidge is worth $1,000,000 a year to the Republican Party." In her memoirs she explained that a stray reporter wandered into the meeting, with the result that produced front-page stories in the *New York Times* and *Washington Post* the next morning and an avalanche of editorials and articles and anonymous letters accusing her, among other things, of "degrading Mrs. Coolidge by putting a money value on her." Next time she saw Mrs. Coolidge at the White House the first lady said, "Well, Vera, we've certainly had a lot of publicity together." "Yes," Vera laughed, "we've had the publicity together, Mrs. Coolidge, but I've had the trouble alone!" In her book she explained, with Knickerbocker frankness, that "Mrs. Coolidge was never beautiful; she wasn't even what you'd call pretty. She just had a pleasant, average face and a slender, average figure; but her genuine interest in you, which shone out through her warm, dark eyes, and her *kindness* (not 'graciousness,' that terrible word!) seemed to cast a sort of glow wherever she went."[29]

Evidence of her charm received testimonials in the last days of February 1929 when a group of women gave her a handsome diamond brooch in recognition of the "tact and charm" with which she filled her responsible position. The brooch was two and one-half inches long and one and one-half wide, with a dazzling five-carat diamond in the center and perfect diamonds on each side totaling three and one-half carats more. Two hundred smaller diamonds were clustered about the others. Along with the brooch came a twenty-two-inch platinum chain, with 170 diamonds set in the bar.[30]

The wives of the senators, many of them members of the Ladies of the Senate she knew in the vice presidency, gave her an antique desk, for which she was once heard to express a wish.[31] An editorial in the *Washington Post* on March 4, 1929, awarded an encomium offered to none of her predecessors: "To Mrs. Coolidge the country gives its heart, which she has fairly won. Throughout the administration Mrs. Coolidge has subordinated self for the sake of duty, with unfailing cheerfulness and charm."

CHAPTER 4

PUBLIC EVENTS

In the five and one-half years the Coolidges spent in the White House, Grace Coolidge's social activities, far beyond those of the vice presidency, required the most exacting attention of any responsibilities she ever undertook during her long life. Let it be said that many of her activities were duties, which she performed as a matter of course—she could not, and did not, question them. Those duties appear in the pages that follow, that is, the White House duties. The others, and there were so many they seem innumerable, she managed partly in the mansion, partly in the city, others whenever she and her husband traveled. As in the case of the White House responsibilities, word of them went out in the newspapers, and frequently the new medium of radio, to people all over the United States, giving further evidence that as first lady she was setting a tone, so to speak, for the nation—and incidentally supporting her husband, who was hard at work as president.

It is a remarkable fact that Grace Coolidge achieved all this with no more experience in Washington than the average tourist. She had been there twice. Her acquaintance began in 1912 when she helped chaperone a visit by the graduating class of Northampton High School. The class toured the sights, among them the public rooms of the White House. In the East Room they saw the ornate grand piano the New York firm of Steinway and Sons had made for the presidents of the United States. Compared with the upright in the entrance to 21 Massasoit Street it was of a different world, tempting to the Northampton housewife, who sat down and began playing. A guard came up—she remembered it a decade and more later—and touched her on the shoulder, asking her to stop. The other visit to Washington occurred in 1916 when Mr. and Mrs. Stearns took the Coolidges to the nation's capital and installed them in the Shoreham Hotel. Frank Stearns wanted them to meet people, and Senator Lodge obliged with a small reception the senator could remember seven years later when Governor Coolidge became president. The Stearnses and Coolidges toured the city, including the first floor of the White House, and Mrs. Coolidge must have seen the piano.

Grace Coolidge sought to share the White House with as many visitors as possible, in every way she could. She received dozens of women during her afternoons, twice a week, Mondays and Wednesdays. Florence Harding gave appointments on an individual basis, of from five to fifteen minutes, but Grace Coolidge felt this was an unworkable arrangement; she never could see all the women who wished to come. She asked wives of government officials to make appointments on Monday afternoons for themselves and friends whom they wished to have received. Wednesday afternoons she received others who asked for appointments. She took them in groups of fifteen, half an hour later another group, and so on until she received all who had asked since the previous Monday or Wednesday. In this way she saw everyone. When all the women, sometimes a brave man or two, who were to be received, say at four o'clock, had arrived, the usher went upstairs to escort her down. Guests were arrayed in a semicircle in the Red Room, and she went in and passed around, pausing to speak with each person in turn. Sometimes two or three who knew one another would be together. After she had gone around, she said good-bye and retired.[1]

Mrs. Coolidge as first lady attempted garden parties, but in the first season two were rained out. Washington weather could turn inclement, and the guests had to be brought into the public rooms, a difficult matter at short notice. In her autobiography she remarked how on both these attempts at parties the sun did come out, and the yard in back, the locale of the parties, glistened with raindrops, making it ever so attractive. But the weather made garden parties inadvisable.

In entertaining at the White House the Coolidges had many houseguests, far more than their predecessors. Excluding relatives, close friends, and administration officials, there were 102 houseguests in five years and seven months. In four years President Taft and his wife had 32 houseguests, in eight years President Wilson had 12, and the Hardings if only because of Florence Harding's illnesses had only 5.[2] Because of the guests the Coolidges were seldom alone for meals, except breakfasts, which Grace Coolidge had served for the two of them in her dressing room. Houseguests had their breakfasts served in their rooms at whatever hour they wished.[3]

Mrs. Coolidge made careful use of the White House greenhouses. Once attached to the mansion, they had been separated in 1902 during the renovation by McKim. The architect hated greenhouses, which he felt detracted from the lines of buildings they served. President Roosevelt wished to "smash the greenhouses."[4] Fortunately, because they were easy to move, what with their iron frames, the architect placed them next to the Bureau of Printing and Engraving; hence plants and flowers were available for decorating rooms of the mansion and in the Coolidge era for sending to friends in bouquets, with cards displaying their origin.

Another use of presidential resources that the Coolidges employed to bolster hospitality was the yacht *Mayflower*. This beautiful ship, carrying a crew of 300 men and officers, had been a private yacht until taken into the navy in 1898 and then relinquished to presidents for their public use. Roosevelt in 1905 employed the saloon of the *Mayflower* to introduce the Russian and Japanese delegations prior to a meeting in Portsmouth, New Hampshire, in which they signed a treaty ending the Russo-Japanese War of 1904–1905.[5] Taft, Wilson, and Harding used the ship mostly for Potomac cruises.

The Coolidge presidency marked the yacht's heyday of use, in which the president and his first lady took much satisfaction. The Potomac cruises, which usually went down into Chesapeake Bay, began on Saturdays. The president made up the guest lists of ten or twelve persons—the yacht had a limited number of guest cabins. Invitations went out by telephone, often at the last moment. Guests assembled at the Washington Navy Yard, and at 2:00 P.M. the presidential party arrived, preceded by a call to the commandant, who relayed word to the captain that the Coolidges were on the way. They passed up the gangplank to the playing of "The Star-Spangled Banner," for which crew and guests stood at attention. The ship weighed anchor and turned into the river. The routine always was the same. As the *Mayflower* approached George Washington's tomb at Mount Vernon, the crew came to attention. In the afternoon a radio aboard ship allowed guests to hear a baseball or football game. At night in good weather there would be a movie shown on the fantail, for everyone interested. Sunday morning there were church services, conducted by a navy chaplain, processional and recessional and hymns accompanied by a string orchestra from the Navy Band. Afterward came the Sunday newspapers, brought in by a navy flying boat, arrival and departure of which was always of interest. Sunday nights the ship anchored off Hains Point, returning to the navy yard the next morning.[6]

The Coolidges were fond of the *Mayflower* and much affected by one of the first acts of their successor in the White House, President Hoover, who decommissioned the yacht and put it up for auction, whereupon it burned. "Did you read in the paper," Grace Coolidge wrote a friend,

> that the dear old *Mayflower* has been seriously burned and rests upon the muddy bed of the Delaware? I can hardly bear it but when Mr. Coolidge told me I said that I was glad. I have hated having her put up at auction and tied up at the wharf, dismantled and rotting. She was a beautiful ship. We have a fine painting of her hanging over the living room mantel. She is pictured off Hains Point, a part of the Potomac Drive, with the Japanese cherry trees in bloom.[7]

Then there were the four annual state dinners, each of which brought a hundred or so people to the White House. The dinner season opened with the cabinet dinner of early December, followed by the diplomatic dinner in mid-December, with the Supreme Court dinner and House Speaker's dinner some weeks later. All state dinners were black tie, smaller dinners (of which there were quite a few) white tie.

The state dinners were sumptuous affairs in which the mansion's best china appeared, with waiters brought in for the occasion and food bounteous as well as best of quality. The New England presidential couple did not serve wine or hard liquor, in consideration of the Eighteenth Amendment that forbade it, nor had their predecessors the Hardings. In every other way the fare at the White House was worthy of the best traditions of the mansion.

In addition there were the musicales. At first Grace Coolidge sought to hold them after the formal dinners, for enjoyment of the guests. It became evident that they should be by themselves, celebrating music at the White House. The world's finest artists played or sang there.[8] During the Coolidge era of White House entertainment a frequent performer, then at the height of his powers (he was the best pianist in the world, as well as a first-rate composer), was Sergei Rachmaninoff. He enjoyed playing for Mrs. Coolidge on the piano in the East Room. He came every time she asked him. The wife of the captain of the *Mayflower,* Mrs. Adolphus Andrews, told Mrs. Coolidge he looked like a convict and played like an angel.[9] One almost can hear him, after eighty years, playing his Prelude in C-sharp Minor of which by that time he probably was tired, but audiences expected it. Of his three performances, that of March 10, 1924, opened with the famous prelude and followed with a Rachmaninoff-adapted "Minuet" by Bizet, then another adapted "Hopak" by Moussorgsky. Thence to "Liebestraum" by Liszt, closing with the latter's Rhapsody no. 2, cadenza by Rachmaninoff. The performance of January 16, 1925, offered "Humoresque" and "Troika" by Tchaikovsky, another "Hopak" by Moussorgsky adapted by the pianist, "Liebeslied" by Fritz Kreisler adapted by Rachmaninoff, a crowd pleaser made famous by the violinist, together with "La Jongleuse" by Moszkowski and a "Faust Fantasy" by Gounod-Liszt— the latter with all of its Lisztean bombast.

The pianist Rudolph Ganz played January 17, 1929, a nocturne and two waltzes and a scherzo by Chopin, closing with Liszt's Polonaise in E Major.

The young violinist Erika Morini appeared March 31, 1924, offering a serenade by Tchaikovsky, a waltz by Brahms, and "Variations on a Theme by Corelli," by Tartini-Kreisler. She shared her program with the baritone John Charles Thomas, who offered songs by Strauss, Wolf, and Brahms.

Singers included the Metropolitan Opera's inimitable Beniamino Gigli, who chose selections from Flotow's *Martha,* Verdi's *Rigoletto,* and songs by Carnivali, Lalo, and Cilea. After Gigli's performance, and others in late afternoons, dinners followed for the artists and guests. Mrs. Coolidge's secretary, Mary Randolph, sat next to Gigli and said to him, "I wish you would sing the whole program over again." With the utmost simplicity the great tenor put his head back and sang and sang, one Italian aria after another, "a golden flood of his voice until it seemed to carry us away to Heaven."[10]

Among singers at the White House was Louise Homer, on January 27, 1927, with Haydn, Schubert, Massenet, Saint-Saëns, and two weeks later, February 10, Elisabeth Rethberg with Brahms, Strauss, Schubert.

The Coolidges brought in cellists, string quartets, harpsichordists, harpists, choral groups, some of the latter perhaps not in the same category as the individual performers, such as the choir of the First Congregational Church in Washington that the first family attended. The president invited the Amherst College glee club. But by and large music at the White House was of a very high order. When John Charles Thomas sang, there was no Gilbert and Sullivan, in which he was an artful performer.[11] The first lady—the president's musical tastes, as he had shown years before when in Boston he made his Chickering Piano Company address, were unknown, probably no better than those of President Ulysses S. Grant, whose favorite selection, though he could not remember it, was "Yankee Doodle"—insisted upon no dumbing down.

And so the Coolidges, with the gracious first lady in the lead, opened the world of music to the American people, introducing them to its virtuosity within the impressive precincts of the White House.

Lastly, and far more important in displaying the grandeur of the presidency and the president's house, were the five annual formal receptions, the diplomatic, judicial, congressional, army and navy, and New Year's Day. In the Coolidge years the receptions alone, apart from the private entertainments, brought between 20,000 and 25,000 people annually to the White House. The New Year's Day receptions were especially large. Begun, strictly by invitation, by President George Washington in New York, they changed during the administration of President Andrew Jackson, who opened them to anyone who wished to come. In 1909, the last year of Theodore Roosevelt's presidency, 10,000 people came. In President

Harding's first New Year's reception 6,500 shook hands with the nation's chief executive and his wife. In the first such reception by President and Mrs. Coolidge there were 3,900; in 1925, there 4,000, with the others averaging 3,000. Attendance varied with the weather, as lines stood outside the White House in a column from the northwest gate of the grounds extending west along Pennsylvania Avenue, thence south on Seventeenth Street along the walk facing what then was the State, War and Navy Building, now the executive offices of the president.

The ceremonial of a reception was usually the same and was very formal.[12] After discontinuance of receptions, and of all social activities for that matter, during American participation in the world war and during the illness of President Wilson, Harding and Coolidge resumed the formalities instituted by Theodore Roosevelt. There were decorations of flowers, great bowls and baskets of them from the greenhouses, placed in vacant spaces on the White House floor. The Marine Orchestra was present in their red coats, and military aides stood about in full dress. The greater number of guests to these receptions came in through the east entrance, checked their wraps on the lower floor, climbed the stairway to the main corridor, from where they were escorted into the East Room. They stood there in line until time for the reception. Members of the cabinet and wives or official hostesses entered the front doors or north porte cochere into the lobby, removed wraps, and were taken up to the private living quarters on the second floor. When they assembled, the president and first lady greeted them. Everyone waited until aides announced time for the reception. In this period the household officials and staff members and certain other personages, such as the army chief of staff, the chief of naval operations, the commandant of the Marine Corps, the commandant of the Coast Guard, with wives or hostesses, gathered in the Blue Room, standard-bearers at each side of the door, facing the lobby—a soldier, sailor, marine, two of them holding the flag of the United States and the presidential flag.

When the hour arrived for the reception, the two senior military aides to the president, army and navy, arrayed in the gold braid that showed them presidential aides, went to the second floor to announce that all was ready. With the president and first lady behind them the aides marched down the grand stairway to the main corridor on the first floor, into the Blue Room, the Marine Orchestra striking up "Hail to the Chief," everyone standing at attention.

The orchestra played throughout the reception and sometimes afterward in the East Room for dancing. Guests coming from the lower floor to the East Room and across the corridor to the dining room usually ranged in fours. As they entered the Red Room they were arranged in twos. Before they reached the Blue Room they went to single file. The Secret Service took station in the East Room and along the corridor and the dining room and Red Room, supervising the procession and looking for anything suspicious, with a second scrutiny as guests narrowed to single file.

Sometimes President Coolidge would be quite gracious, have a pleasant smile or nod or word as people went through. Others he was bored by the hours of hand shaking and showed it by pulling guests across in front of him. Former president Taft saw it and wrote to a friend that "Coolidge is Coolidge and he does the pump-handle work without much grace." His Secret Service guard, Colonel Starling, noticed the pump handle and instructed the president not to do it, but he must not have been at later receptions or he would have seen the pump at work.[13]

Coolidge could be rude to individuals he disliked and seems to have had it in for dowagers with airs. Boone saw one lady coming down the line who caught the president's attention. She was a sweet little woman in a plain black silk dress, lace collar and lace cuffs, wearing a full skirt that made her look dignified. Boone thought her out of an earlier period, translated into the 1920s. She left the Red Room and approached the president, wetting her lips and preparing to make a little speech. She took the president's hand and held her full skirt as she bowed and curtsied, expecting he would respond warmly. He did not look at her at all, pulled her by him with his right hand, looking over his shoulder to the coming guests. When the little lady rose from her curtsey she said, "You know, Mr. President, I am from Boston," this in a New England accent. Without changing his expression the president, looking beyond her, said, "Madam, you will never get over it." When Mrs. Stearns later that evening or the next day asked Coolidge if the story about this greeting were true he said in his nasal way, "You can vouch for it."

According to Starling, when the president espied a dowager in line he would nudge the colonel and say, "Colonel, stop the line at that lady there. I've got to rest." While the lady waited, he would go and sit down for five or ten minutes.

Mrs. Coolidge tempered her husband's pump handle and other acts of misbehavior at receptions by greeting visitors with a broad smile and firm handshake and a word or two or more if she knew them. If she thought the president was rushing guests through, she would move several paces away from him, increasing the distance, to give more time for her greetings. The president was aware of this and would close up the gap. After a little while, biding her time, she would again separate herself. It was amusing to watch this minuet.

One might ask why the president behaved at receptions as if he wished to get them over, and misbehaved with the dowagers. The latter probably was because of his Yankee origins and representation of Amherst College against the Boston Back Bay. He also was bored, and as president felt he was entitled to show it. He and his far more gracious wife nonetheless believed that as dwellers, temporary dwellers in the People's House, they should show appreciation to Americans who, after all, owned the house. Beyond gratitude, more important, was the need to dignify the presidency. Their hospitality, most often in holding the gigantic White House receptions, honored the presidency they both revered and the house representing that institution.

In addition to Grace Coolidge's formal duties in the White House, the at homes and dinners and receptions and myriad, it must have seemed, ways of the mansion's hospitality there was a constant kaleidoscopic participation of appearances of people in the White House or the first lady's work elsewhere, almost all of it announced to the watching public near and afar. The mere fact that Grace Coolidge was a college woman brought interest, although the once undergraduate student, not always a good one, at the university in Burlington did not stand for what onlookers considered it. A discerning woman, Winifred Carr, wrote in the *New York Times*, which published the letter, of how a college education did not necessarily prove much. An editorial in the newspaper had attributed Mrs. Coolidge's college degree as the chief source of her ability and charm. "I believe," was the letter of response, "that Grace Coolidge would have been quite as charming, tactful and capable without college training. These characteristics are part of her personality and could not have been acquired through the medium of college materials." The writer knew many college women who remained very ordinary individuals. Individuality could not be acquired at college. "Grace Coolidge has it. She is well named. Grace sits upon her brow."[14]

College presidents nonetheless sought to stress the degree, one suspects to advertise their institutions as well as what their students might do. Early in Grace Coolidge's time as first lady, the president of Oberlin College in Ohio, Henry Churchill King, his ability confirmed by his middle name, came to Washington and the first lady disposed of him by planting a tree in the grounds of the Lincoln Memorial at noon, November 25, 1923, in a drizzling rain. Mrs. Coolidge used a spade once used by Edith Roosevelt, who planted a tree at the White House.[15] The first lady received an honorary doctorate of law from Boston University, the connection being that the university was in Boston. The convocation met in the Old South Church, and she was accompanied by Captain Andrews of the *Mayflower*. The citation was suitably rotund: "Grace Goodhue Coolidge—student, university graduate, teacher, daughter, wife, mother; in every station exemplifying the finer qualities of mind and heart we most admire in woman; your own works praise you; you have gained the confidence, admiration and love of the American people." The ceremony caught national attention, and the first lady received a hood of purple, with trimmings of red and white.[16] In Burlington, on June 19, 1926, Mrs. Coolidge was present at the unveiling of her portrait by the artist Alexius de Laszlo de Lombos, presented to the university by Darwin P. Kingsley of New York City.[17] President and Mrs. Coolidge received honorary degrees from George Washington University on February 22, 1929.[18] After the first lady and her husband left Washington to return to Northampton, she received degrees from Smith College and from her Burlington alma mater.

Undoubtedly the first lady's close connection with the Pi Phis of Burlington produced the most remarkable tribute to her college education, this in a presentation in the East Room in April 1924.[19] The Pi Phis of Michigan together with those of Massachusetts raised $3,000 to pay the fee of the painter Howard Chandler Christy, who

chose a remarkable scene for Mrs. Coolidge—standing in front of
the White House, with her favorite white collie dog on a leash. She
wore a simple red dress, which gave rise to a story, probably true,
about a suggestion from her presidential husband who wished her
to wear his favorite white dress. Christy pointed out that everything
thus would be white, and her husband said, with his Vermont
straight face, "Paint the dog red." The portrait was far and away the
best done of the first lady during the White House years, a gorgeous
likeness, a bit elongated in the usual way. For the unveiling hundreds
of Pi Phis came to Washington. Mrs. Coolidge estimated attendance
in the East Room at 3,000, doubtless confusing it with the fee, but
there could have been half that number. On the day of the unveiling
the fraternity's gold arrows were everywhere. All the grand officers
were present, and Anna Robinson Nickerson, who held the distinc-
tion of being both a robin and the grand vice president, offered a
statement: "From the days of Martha Washington until now never
has it [the federal government] had as the wife of its President a
woman more universally admired and loved. It seems distinctly fit-
ting that to Pi Beta Phi . . . has come the signal honor of claiming as
its own Grace Goodhue Coolidge, first lady of the land." Mrs. Coolidge appeared in soft gray georgette crepe trimmed with crystal, and
wore a jeweled eagle on her shoulder, a chain with crystal pendant, a
gold bracelet, and of course the Pi Phi arrow, a diamond-studded
one she received the day before from a group of friends to replace
the pin with opals she had worn since college days. Representatives
of Vermont Beta and Michigan Alpha drew the silver-blue cords.

The curtain, wine-blue, parted. Colonel Clarence G. Sherrill, cus-
todian of the White House, accepted the gift. The Marine Band
played. Everyone sang the fraternity anthem. The group moved into
the Blue Room and afterward toured the other public rooms and the
grounds, the latter abloom in springtime garb of magnolias, and in
the beds thousands of pansies, jonquils, and crocuses.

The alumnae club of Washington sold copies of the painting for
the benefit of the fraternity's settlement school in Tennessee. Repli-
cas sold for four dollars. Those autographed by Mrs. Coolidge sold
for a dollar extra. The present writer has one, duly framed, covered
with light-resistant glass, received from his aunt whose intimate
friend was a Michigan Pi Phi. Mrs. Coolidge dated it April 16, 1924.

Mrs. Coolidge was no joiner—similar in that way to her husband, who thought a politician was no person to join every local or national organization offering membership. The first lady through her social secretary, if necessary through her own agency, stayed away from the organizations that before and after the world war proliferated throughout America. She did join the Washington College Women's Club, perhaps difficult to remain apart from. She studiously stayed away from the Daughters of the American Revolution, which had a connection with an experience she and her husband had with the DAR in 1905, after they had returned from the wedding trip to Montreal. Arriving back in Northampton, they went to a reception at the Academy of Music for the governor of the state and his lady by the local DAR chapter. Chairs were duly ringed around the room, and the newlyweds sat down in two of them, only to be told by someone that those chairs were reserved for the governor and wife. Embarrassed, irritated, they never forgot the incident, and when Coolidge became governor a dozen or so years later, one of the first things he said to his wife was that at last they would be able to sit in the governor's chairs and no DAR members could get them out.

More likely the cause of the first lady's aversion to organizations including specifically the DAR was that as her husband rose in politics they both were terribly busy and had no time. Mrs. Coolidge also told Boone on one occasion that she had no use for organizations based on forebears, thought them silly. She nonetheless was highly eligible for the DAR if only from her father's lineage, the Goodhues, probably also her maternal grandfather's line, the Barretts. As her husband's political fortunes rose, the pressure to join mounted, and the registrar of the Massachusetts branch of the DAR, Mary A. Todd, on March 18, 1921, declared her a life member.[20] Nothing more came of this announcement, no move at all on the part of the new life member. But when 5,000 DAR members descended on Washington, undoubtedly something of a spectacle, the Coolidges received them at the White House, this on April 24, 1925. They treated them to a lawn party. Earlier that day they received the Children of the Revolution, some in quaint colonial costume.[21]

For national children's groups such as the Girl Scouts and Campfire Girls the no-joining policy had to be relaxed. On May 9, 1926, the first lady, wearing the uniform of the Scouts, received fifty or more at noon in the Blue Room, delegates from thirty-nine countries who came from New York for a day's visit to Washington. On leaving the White House the visitors and a large local group went to the new Scout Waffle Shop on F Street for luncheon. For the Girl Scouts the wife of the secretary of commerce in the Coolidge cabinet, Lou Henry Hoover, had been an active advocate, and if only for that reason Grace Coolidge almost had to participate now and then.[22] On one occasion Mrs. Hoover arranged to interview the first lady on events of her youth in Burlington, and an article appeared in the national Scout magazine. Similarly, the first lady was honorary chair of the national advisory committee of Campfire Girls, and on March 12, 1926, received a ceremonial robe and headbands from a delegation representing the Campfire Girls of the country, and also received the name of Ailayi, which signified first lady of the land. The robe marked the fourteenth anniversary of the Campfire Girls and was the gift of more than 100,000 members. Around the bottom of the gown were symbols, a ship with rays of sun behind, for the east, a pine tree for the north, and the sun for the south. Around the collar the seven points of the Campfire law were represented. On the right sleeve was a symbol of the primitive woman.[23]

One organization, indeed two of them, she joined with enthusiasm, both being baseball clubs. Throughout her life her passion for the sport never diminished. She gave attention as first lady to football, as when on November 20, 1926, she watched the army and navy, the latter represented by the marines, play at Catholic University in Washington. She suitably was neutral between the two branches of the military. It was actually not a national match but between a group from Fort Benning and another from Quantico. The marines won, 27 to 7.[24] Ostensibly she sided with neither team, sitting with the navy the first half, the army the second, but one suspected her allegiance was with Quantico because of the contingent of marines stationed aboard the *Mayflower* with whom she was altogether friendly. As for serious interest her attention was on baseball, and here she was known everywhere in America as the First Lady of Baseball.[25] No other first lady had shown or would show such an intense interest. During her years in Washington her team was the Senators. Upon return to Northampton it was the Boston Red Sox.

This love affair with America's premier sport during the 1920s, and for long afterward, was no pose to assist her political husband, whose interest in any sport, local or national, was modest to the point of demonstrated indifference. One could tell it when he annually threw out the first ball to the Senators on their home turf. With all the local team's dignitaries and leading players surrounding him, everyone smiling, his wife beaming, he tossed out the ball with an imperceptible overhand motion as if it were a distasteful object containing a small bomb, whereupon everyone cheered as if he had done something. This was quickly evident in the sort of passes the two Coolidges received. No longer did the former vice president, virtually unknown but now president and internationally a figure to enthusiasts of the game everywhere, receive passes from both national leagues bearing the wrong middle initials. His pass was the usual folder variety containing a monogram mounting. The vice president beginning March 1925, General Dawes, received a similar folder entitling him to walk into any American League park without the need of visiting the ticket seller. Mrs. Coolidge received with the league's compliments a most elaborate pass, in the form of the popular envelope purse, of pin seal mounted with a gold monogram, "G.G.C." The purse contained a leather-bound schedule for the season and a container for small change.[26]

The Coolidges attended one game together in October 1924 in which the unlucky Senators played the New York Giants. In the exciting ninth inning Walter Johnson pitched, and the score tied 3 to 3. The first lady leaned forward to watch, her eyes never missing a play. A story, perhaps apocryphal, had it that her husband shifted uneasily, and suddenly he rose to leave, but his wife seized his coattails with the injunction, "Where do you think you're going? Calvin, you sit down!" According to the story, he sat down. When the president and first lady watched the extra innings and the Senators defeated the Giants, winning the world championship, the first lady screamed with the rest of the fans.[27] Years later Grace Coolidge attended games of the Sox in Boston, otherwise avidly listening over the radio (see chapter 7).

In an evening father-and-son banquet at the Edwards Church on November 11, 1948, the featured speaker was Joe Coleman, the Philadelphia Athletics' pitcher. A youth asked him whether anyone ever made an unassisted triple play in a world series. The pitcher stuttered and finally admitted he was stumped. Mrs. Coolidge, in the audience, quietly gave him the answer: "Yes, Bill Wambsganss, Cleveland infielder, in the 1920 series."[28]

In Washington the Coolidges attended the wedding of Mary Elizabeth Sutherland and the Senators' "boy wonder" manager, Stanley "Bucky" Harris. The latter later moved to Boston and the Sox, where the general manager, Joe Cronin, and his special assistant and Harris upon Grace Coolidge's death fondly recalled her interest. She was "a wonderful woman," they said, "and the most rabid baseball fan of any presidents' wives." "I first met her when I was playing with the Washington ball club," Cronin said. "She used to go to a great many games there. And after I came to Boston she was one of our finest rooters."[29]

In the Coolidge years almost anything the first lady did or bore even the slightest connection with got into the newspapers or in shortened form appeared on the radio. The era marked rapidly increasing interest in gardening, of which Mrs. Coolidge had been an admirer if not a large participant because of the confines of the lot at the side and in back of 21 Massasoit Street and her own busyness with the family in the last few years before the move to Washington and the vice presidency. When she arrived in the White House, flowers were named after her, notably the ever-expanding varieties of roses. A new "Mrs. Coolidge rose" almost at once made its appearance. The feature of the twenty-ninth flower show of the Tarrytown (New York) Horticultural Society show, which opened at the local YMCA on October 31, 1923, shown by thc F. R. Pierson Company, was the rose. It had no thorns on the stem and deepened into a rich orange color. Nearly all yellow roses heretofore developed bleach as they opened, and this one did not. The company had been developing the rose for a year and carefully wrote to the first lady beforehand and obtained her consent to use her name. John D. Rockefeller had to take third place in the chrysanthemum group, as compared with the distinctive rose.[30] At the show of the American Horticultural Society in Washington on June 8, 1926, the first lady was presented with a bouquet of Mrs. Calvin Coolidge roses. She was accompanied by the wife of Vice President Dawes and by Alice Roosevelt Longworth, wife of Speaker Nicholas Longworth of the House of Representatives. The Washington show exhibited 128 varieties of flowers; in the afternoon the Marine Band played, presumably in their bright red uniforms, and in the evening the Marine Band Orchestra.[31]

An Indiana grower, A. E. Kundred, known as the gladiolus wizard of Goshen, Indiana, won first prize for an unnamed bloom at an exhibition at Hartford, Connecticut, and named it in honor of the first lady of the land.

Mrs. Coolidge, meanwhile, dealt with the awkward problem of what to do when people asked for gifts for charitable purposes, such as auctioning them off. Either Miss Harlan or Miss Randolph, it might have been Mrs. Coolidge, hit on a solution that offered a diplomatic, little-price-or-trouble-involved donation, but then they did not stick with it. A steel-engraving picture of the White House, bearing the signature of Mrs. Coolidge, went to Hugh C. Gambel, chairman of the general commission in charge of raising funds for a memorial monument to be erected in East Rockaway, Long Island. Mrs. Coolidge enclosed a letter of transmission. Apparently she had intended to stop the practice of other presidents' wives in sending handkerchiefs and baby clothes when called upon to contribute money to funds. Mrs. Coolidge's gift was to be auctioned at a block party.[32]

The exceptions to the gift rule thus established may have ended this promising try to end a nuisance afflicting first ladies before 1923–1929. Only the community of Sea Cliff, Long Island, which may have heard of the earlier gift to East Rockaway, applied for another steel engraving, or somehow it made its way there. This was for the benefit of the Nassau Hospital at Mineola.[33] Later the little Methodist Episcopal Church in Long Lake, New York, was richer by $100 through the generosity of the first lady. The forty-nine members decided to conduct a fair for funds to carry on their work, and the first lady sent a gracious note and a photograph of the White House taken by herself, bearing an autograph, which sold to a summer guest for $100.[34] The American Shakespeare Foundation, on Nassau Street in New York City, received a scroll bearing the name of Grace Coolidge, with a sum of money, undisclosed, to place toward the $1 million the foundation hoped to raise for the of the $2.5 million international fund to rebuild and endow the burned Shakespeare Memorial Theatre at Stratford-on-Avon. The scroll, duly described in the *New York Times,* had been signed by the members of the chapter of Phi Beta Kappa at the University of Vermont, of which Mrs. Coolidge had been a member, and sent to her with a space left vacant at the top for her signature. Transmitted, it then would become a part of the archives of the Shakespeare Memorial Library.[35] The requests for something eleemosynary must have come into the White House in a constant stream. On February 1, 1929, just in time to catch the first lady before she gave up her post, a fund for purchasing a new Bible for the Methodist Episcopal Church at Coxetown, near Harrisburg, Pennsylvania, received a $2 addition from Mrs. Coolidge. Mrs. Flora Peiffer of Lucknow, teacher of a boys' Sunday school class, which offered to raise the money to purchase the Bible, made the gift known. The boys had sent out envelopes arranged so the contributor could insert ten dimes. One went to Mrs. Coolidge at the White House. The inventive Miss Randolph, in the name of the first lady, or Mrs. Coolidge may have done it herself, inserted ten new dimes in the envelope and a check for $1, signed Grace Coolidge.[36]

Miss Randolph effectively enlarged Mrs. Coolidge's appearances in newspapers by answering with care the letters she received from the first lady's small acts of consideration and kindness. Typical of what must have been hundreds, perhaps even thousands, of tactful letters were two missives sent before and after Mrs. Coolidge spent the summer of 1927 in the Black Hills on vacation with her husband. When the first lady passed through East Chicago in Indiana, she assisted in dedicating the Wicker Memorial Park of Hammond and received a letter of thanks from Mayor Raleigh P. Hale. Mary Randolph sent a letter of response: "I deeply appreciate your kind message and that of your administration, and I thank you for your beautiful flowers. Please accept my best wishes for yourself and for all the citizens of your city." This appeared in the *New York Times* on June 29, 1927. During the vacation Mrs. Coolidge received from Mrs. Stover of Denver the special candy that the Denver entrepreneur sent from her Bungalow Stores, and the message of thankfulness remarked, "Everybody is so kind to us that we should be queer folks indeed if we were not having a good time. But we are having more than that, and when we return to Washington we shall be refreshed and strengthened by the friendliness of the people and the hills."

Presumably the thriving candy enterprise, which lasted long into the future throughout the West and Midwest, and the people of those expansive regions were pleased to know this news, suitably printed for the East in the *New York Times*.[37]

Annually the issue arose of Christmas trees for the White House and who would decorate them. In 1926 a new arrangement came into being, not a single tree at the White House but three, the idea of the first lady. These were inside trees, inside the mansion. She determined to have them on the first floor rather than the second, the private living quarters. They arrived on December 22 and were to be erected the next day. Her first choice was the Blue Room, the White House's formal reception room. If she decided not to place all the trees in this room, she would have one in the Green Room and the other in the Red Room, which flanked the Blue Room. Decorating the trees would fall to the first lady and her son John, at home from Amherst College, where he was a junior, to spend Christmas with his parents. Mr. and Mrs. Frank W. Stearns, who had been spending a month as guests in the White House, might assist in the tree trimming (an unlikely assumption for the department store owner, who was stout and sedentary). Mrs. Coolidge prided herself at being something of an expert in trimming and had determined not to turn over the task to others, for, she said, it had always given her so much pleasure. The president would have little to do with the trimming but would offer suggestions. The White House trees would be trimmed with tinsel, brightly colored ornaments, electrically lighted candles (the Coolidges' successors, the Franklin Roosevelts, used, for that president liked them, regular candles, a scary project for any Christmas tree). At the bottom of each of the Coolidges' trees in 1926 would be highly colored figures of Santa Claus. Christmas presents were arriving from all parts of the country, not merely from friends and relatives but from unknown well-wishers. Greeting cards arrived into the thousands. That year the president agreed to light the community Christmas tree in Sherman Square to the rear of the White House grounds. There were to be carols from the front portion of the White House by the choir of the First Congregational Church of Washington.[38]

Indeed, stories in honor of the charming first lady filled the papers day after day, to a point almost beyond belief, and one suspects that whether inspired by people she touched or by her wonderfully alert social secretaries in the alcove above the front door of the mansion, they amounted to more than any of those about first ladies before her and probably after, with the exception of Eleanor Roosevelt, whose endless activities defied imagination. Mary Randolph thought so and related the fact in her *Presidents and First Ladies.*

In all this Grace Coolidge made many people happy and constituted a most useful foil to the dour personality of her far less attractive husband—which surely she knew about, and although hers was no calculating nature must have been included in her thoughts, day to day.

CHAPTER 5

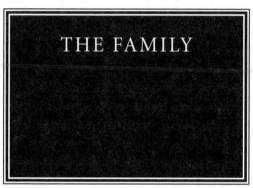

THE FAMILY

Grace Goodhue Coolidge, wife of the thirtieth president of the United States, 1923–1929, was the envy of millions of Americans as in the newspaper accounts of the great receptions in the White House she came down the stairway of the mansion in the company of her husband the president. It was a role that suited her, a woman who possessed modesty, intelligence, and her presiding national quality, charm. To all appearances her life symbolized what a first lady should be. Her lot in life, people said, fitted perfectly with what the nation's voters would have assigned her, if they could have done such a thing.

And yet her years in Washington as wife of Calvin Coolidge constituted hardly the perfection that the public beheld; for one of those years saw the deepest of sorrows, the tragic death of her younger son, Calvin Jr., in 1924, and in the next two years of her husband's presidency, 1925 and 1926, and part of 1927, the middle years of their time in Washington, relations between them, their private lives, were distressingly poor. It was the old trouble, but the wrong solution. During her husband's rise to the governorship of Massachusetts she had been a safety valve, a balance wheel able to help with release of his personal tensions. This time he refused to allow her to help, went his own lonely way. He ignored her and often was rude. After the death of Calvin Jr., he made everything worse by his inability to deal with their son John, who was a thoroughly normal youth growing into manhood, and needing the friendship rather than the rigid supervision of his father.

The first months of the presidency saw her husband snappish with the boys, but Grace Coolidge for the most part continued to handle them at Mercersburg Academy in Pennsylvania, where in the autumn of 1921 they had transferred from the Northampton public schools. Then came the death of Calvin Jr., a terrible experience for both senior Coolidges, after which—a bad omen for family life—they showed inability to communicate about their misery. Both resorted to religion but could not talk about it.

In subsequent years, 1925 and into 1927, each containing a three-month vacation when the president and wife were thrown together awkwardly, family relations reached a distinct low. Fortunately, it was invisible to the general public; both Coolidges being very private people, no word got out, except to Dr. Boone, who kept Grace Coolidge's confessions to himself. The only news of family trouble was the so-called Haley affair at the beginning of the Black Hills vacation in 1927, which received newspaper publicity, though not a great deal of it.

At this point, in midsummer 1927, typically, the president mulled over in his mind, but did not tell his wife, what to do about his inability to handle the pressing problems of his presidency—political, economic, foreign—and maintain a sound marriage. He decided his presidency was of lesser importance than getting along with his wife and son John, that he could take no more of it. The result was a political bombshell, as it was described, his announcement of August 2, 1927, the anniversary of President Harding's death and his own accession to the presidency, that he would not run as he could have, in 1928. The decision much pleased his wife—and Secretary of Commerce Hoover, whose political manager, Secretary of the Interior Hubert Work, at once seized the initiative across the country and began gathering delegates for the 1928 Republican convention, the same way as Senator William M. Butler of Massachusetts gathered votes for Coolidge in 1923–1924. Coolidge gave appearance of desiring a draft in 1928 but stuck to his decision. He found it reinforced when early in 1928 his wife came down with a serious case of kidney disease. In the next months the virtual estrangement between father

Rob Roy stretches for Grace's handkerchief, September 26, 1924,
three and a half months after Calvin Jr.'s death.
Courtesy of the Forbes Library, Northampton, Massachusetts.

and son, the president and John, gradually lessened, assisted by the pretty daughter of Governor John Trumbull of Connecticut at Mount Holyoke College near Amherst, where John was finishing college. Everything turned almost tranquil as the presidential years ended, with the family—agonizing though the experience had been—back together.

The two Coolidge boys spent the spring semester of 1921 in Northampton, looked after by Mrs. Reckahn and Mrs. Hills down the street, and duly enrolled at Mercersburg that fall. During that time their mother kept in close touch, and there was an amusing reminder from Calvin Jr. that he told her she owed him money because he had received good grades.[1] The amount in question was thirty-three cents. That spring she talked with Boone about Mercersburg Academy, of which he was an ardent alumnus, and she visited it, looked over the dormitories, and talked with the headmaster and wife. She arranged for the boys to go there in August 1921, when John would be in the tenth grade and Calvin Jr. the eighth. The boys meanwhile visited there. John wrote his mother that if he had a boy he would put him in Mercersburg.[2] Calvin Jr. was laconic, and too young to testify about having a boy.

When John and Calvin Jr. arrived at Mercersburg, they roomed together, a convenient arrangement, and they and their mother chose furniture and the rugs to bring down from Northampton. Reactions to the first day were different. John wrote, "I am awfully lonesome and I didn't sleep good last night. I wish I were at home. I was sorry to see you go away, mother." The same day the letter arrived in Washington there was a second letter, written the same evening, with a different story:

We went in the swimming pool this afternoon—I'm having a swell time. You couldn't pry me away now. I have gotten acquainted with several boys. Classes begin tomorrow. Our rugs came this evening and I have them down. Looks fine. There are many fine boys here. Probably you have a letter from me already. I felt lonesome and "bawled." I don't know why I did but I just felt like it. Mercersburg is a nice little town. I hope you will come up to see us sometime.

Calvin Jr., younger, was less lonely and fitted in.

Everything is going finely. Work begins tomorrow. We went in the swimming pool today. The man we got the locker of went to a college in Springfield, Massachusetts and so he knew all about Northampton. The boys are very pleasant and nice here. They all offer to help us if we want anything. We have become friends of those two boys from Philadelphia. You met them, their mother was dressed in black. Football practice started this afternoon. There is a football game the Saturday after now. We will have a good team, I guess. We are having a very good time and hope you are.[3]

With such boys, unspoiled, their father was unable to relate, evident in a letter he wrote Calvin Jr. just before they enrolled. He referred at the onset to his younger son's summer work in the fields near Northampton where Calvin Jr. was cutting tobacco:

We hope you are getting on all right in your work in the fields. I do not know whether your mother will be able to go up to Northampton to pick up some of the things that are there which we want down here. We are all right and always glad to hear from you, but I am too busy just now [he was writing on August 14, 1921] to say anything other than that we want you to keep on in being a good boy and doing your school work.[4]

During the time the boys were in Mercersburg, 1921–1924, their mother was in touch. Especially during the presidency their father was remote, except when they came to Washington for vacations and he told them what to do in regard to trivial points of behavior, concerning which he should have deferred to his wife. He made them eat dinner in the state dining room in tuxedos. He told them when they should wear their rubbers and insisted that they wear galluses, suspenders, rather than belts. He supervised clothes. The boys brought home new suits and other items they liked and asked Boone about them, and the doctor agreed with their choices. Everything rested with their father, and the boys left the clothes laid out, suits on the bed, hats on the dresser, until their father came over from the executive offices for lunch. Coolidge had the boys try on the clothes and did not ask them what ones they liked. He pointed at one suit for John and said, "You will take that one, John." Then he said, "Calvin, you will take that one." He applied the same instruction to the hats, turned quickly, and left the room.[5]

Then, July 2, 1924, tragedy struck, when the president and Mrs. Coolidge learned, at first a little uncertainly, that Calvin Jr. was in physical trouble. Just a few days earlier the four Coolidges had posed standing in front of a goldfish pool in the south grounds of the White House, and it was so evident that within a bare year, 1923–1924, Calvin Jr. had grown a foot or more, reaching the height of his older brother. He was such a handsome young man, thin and delicate in his face, clearly like his father, reminiscent (for anyone who had seen the

The president and first lady after the 1924 election.
Courtesy of the Forbes Library, Northampton, Massachusetts.

few photographs of Coolidge's mother) of the delicate face of Victoria Josephine Moor Coolidge. It was a beautiful day, everyone standing there. In a moment, it seemed, everything was gone.

Boone described the illness of young Calvin in his memoirs from the day, July 2, when the doctor had gone out to the tennis courts behind the White House to play doubles with the boys and the Secret Service agent assigned to Mrs. Coolidge, James Haley.[6] Only John and Haley were there. He asked, and they told him Calvin Jr. was not feeling well and was upstairs on the second floor of the White House, probably lying on a bed. The doctor went up and found Grace Coolidge playing the piano and the younger boy stretched out on a bed as they said. His temperature, it turned out, was 102. His responses to questions were "nope" and "yup." To an inquiry he responded that he did have a blister on a toe, obtained two days earlier when in a hurry to play tennis on the White House court he had gone out without wearing socks. Boone saw the blister, saw it was infected and that there were streaks on Calvin's leg, a bad sign.

Consultations followed, and on July 5 the boy was taken to Walter Reed Hospital, where his case rapidly worsened. It was clear that he was suffering from *Staphylococcus aureus,* spreading in a massive septicemia, for which at that time there was no cure. His breathing became labored, and oxygen was brought in. His heart faltered, he became unconscious, and died on July 7.

The Coolidges went out to Walter Reed and stayed in a room across the hall from that of their son. As Boone watched from the head of the bed, the president pulled out a locket and pressed it in the hand of his son; the locket contained a lock of sandy-red hair of the president's mother. The boy was conscious and grasped the locket, dropped it upon losing consciousness, the president again placed it in his hand, to no avail, and the third time held it in the boy's hand while he stroked his head in affection. In this way Calvin Jr. died. Mrs. Coolidge came from across the hall to gaze, with her husband, at their son lying there in death. They said nothing, simply looked. They crossed the hall to the room, thanked the physicians and nurses, and went back to the White House.

There was a simple service in the East Room, which was filled with flowers sent from dozens of people, from heads of state to individual citizens. At Northampton there was another service at the Edwards Church, followed by burial in the family plot at the Notch.

Afterward newspapers published letters Calvin Jr. wrote that showed his essential modesty and underlined his attractiveness. One was to a boy who had written to him upon his father's becoming president, describing him as the first boy of the land. Calvin had written back, "I think you are mistaken in calling me the first boy of the land since I have done nothing. It is my father who is president.

Rather the first boy of the land would be some boy who had distinguished himself through his own actions." Another was to a boy who had said that if his father were president of the United States he would not be working in the tobacco fields near Northampton. Calvin's answer was, "If your father was my father, you would."[7]

To the experience of seeing Calvin die, and learning of these posthumously revealed letters, the Coolidge parents reacted differently. Grace Coolidge wrote the robins, "No longer can we see and touch Calvin but in a very real sense this year he taught me to swim—not because I wanted to learn but just because he wanted to teach me. He put his hand under my chin and I just had to do my best to please him. I'll never forget how happy he was when I took a few strokes, and heard his encouraging voice and I am not going to disappoint him."[8] She wore white as mourning for Calvin, not black. She resorted to poetry, based on the faith of her fathers:

> A charge to keep I have,
> A God to glorify,
> A never-dying soul to save,
> And fit it for the sky.

She wrote this to Boone in 1927 when Boone's mother died. "There was," she said, "no separation possible between His children and in walking closely to God we have also the companionship of His Saints in Glory—your mother, my boy."[9] One of her poems spoke of the small Coolidge plot at the Notch where her son lay.

> Within a green-roofed house, sweet memories blessing every room,
> Across the road, a small white church whose open door invites to prayer.
> And, just around the turn, on yonder hill, God's plot.
> Where sleep His dead and mine beneath two guardian pines.[10]

The president suffered alone, and although there was evidence of enormous grief, he held it to himself.[11] The night before the service in the East Room he came down into the room in a dressing gown and stood before the casket and stroked his son's hair, a heartrending scene. A letter came from his old enemy Senator Lodge.[12] Beneath Lodge's prejudices the senator was as tenderhearted as the president and wrote of the death of his own son years before, in

1909. The two Lodges had been together on a remote and lonely island, and the son died suddenly in the father's arms, of a stroke or
heart attack. There is no record of an answer to his letter, but Coolidge saved it, and it was in a small group of letters discovered in the
attic of the house at the Notch many years later. Long after
Coolidge's death a letter to Colonel Coolidge, ailing at the Notch on
December 9, 1925, revealed how he felt: "It is getting to be almost
Christmas time again. I always think of mother and Abbie and
grandmother and now of Calvin. Perhaps you will see them all before I do, but in a little while we shall all be together for Christmas."[13] In the well-known passage about Calvin Jr. in his autobiography the president mentioned the ways of Providence but laid the
blame on his high office: "If I had not been President he would not
have raised a blister on his toe, which resulted in blood poisoning,
playing lawn tennis in the South Grounds." He added what seemed
rueful words: "I do not know why such a price was exacted for occupying the White House."[14]

The White House mailman, who distributed incoming mail, Ira
R. T. Smith, was sorting mail one day when he came on a letter from
a woman with a small son who said she wanted to know what church
the president would attend and at what time he would be there. She
was in Washington only a few days and wanted her son to get a
glimpse of the president. She asked if she might have a telephone call
at her hotel. The letter was special delivery. Smith noticed that Coolidge was standing beside him, and he handed the president the letter.
Coolidge read it carefully and, without saying anything, picked up a
pencil and wrote, "Phone 10:30 A.M. Monday." He went away abruptly.
This meant he would see her and her son that Monday at the given
time.[15] Then there was the small boy who pressed himself against the
White House fence and looked toward the mansion when by chance
Starling came along and inquired what he wanted. He said he wished
to see the president and say how sorry he was that Calvin Jr. had died.
Starling carried the message. Coolidge saw him, and afterward told
Starling never to refuse any small boy who wished to see him.[16]

The trouble with the summers of 1925 and 1926 and the first part of
the vacation of 1927 arose because of the heavy burdens of the presidency. Coolidge's first year saw his easy nomination and certain

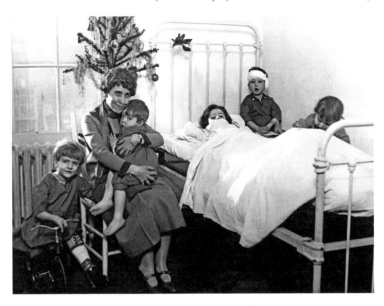

Children's Hospital, Washington, D.C.
Courtesy of the Forbes Library, Northampton, Massachusetts.

election against the Democrats' ineffectual nominee (after 103 ballots), the Wall Street lawyer John W. Davis. Pressure on the presidency thereafter, domestic and foreign, was incessant, rousing him to a state of nerves and bad humor. He was overworked. In the Northampton and Boston years he handled these situations, admittedly of far less importance, by relying on his wife to help him unwind, but in 1925–1927 he did not do so. Why he did not is impossible to say; it may have started with his willingness to stand apart from her despite his intense grief over the death of Calvin Jr. He did not take the vacations as opportunities to seek her help; indeed, until after the opening days of the vacation of 1927 he kept to himself, with the result that the vacations of 1925, 1926, and 1927 until after the Haley affair were family disasters.

The choice for a vacation in 1925 was White Court, a low, rambling house near Swampscott, Massachusetts, near the house, Red Gables, of Mr. and Mrs. Stearns. The principal reason for choosing it was proximity to Plymouth Notch, where the president's father was suffering from a kidney ailment and needed visits; the elder Coolidge died in 1926. Offhand White Court seemed what the president and wife needed, for it was in their beloved Massachusetts and near the shore, with a green yard that sloped down to the rocks, in which were two pools for freshwater bathing and a small beach for hardy souls who wished to sunbathe or wade in the cold salt water. The *Mayflower* could dock three miles away in a cove at Little Neck, from whence the inhabitants of White Court might take short trips and could sit on deck and watch sailboat races. The executive offices were nearby in the town of Lynn. The president did not much use the offices, preferring to do business at White Court, where cabinet and other officers from Washington came and went.[17]

Offhand the arrangement at White Court seemed fine, but there were drawbacks, one being that for both the president and his wife there were no places to walk other than in Swampscott, where their presence attracted onlookers. The other was that John Coolidge, home from Amherst, studying French, which he detested, was under a ban about socializing from his father who was disturbed by his son's first college year. The French turned young John in the direction of rebellion.

The president, Grace Coolidge believed, had learned little from his experiences with their older son. She did not say it but evidently thought the searing experience of Calvin Jr.'s death had not softened the father, made him see the older son was sensitive and needed consideration rather than a ban on social life. During a trip of the *Mayflower* to the Boston Navy Yard the mother talked with the president's secretary, former congressman Everett Sanders of Indiana, and Dr. Boone. She said she would prefer to use the "barge," meaning the *Mayflower,* to make trips along the coast so they could stop here and there and go ashore. She would like to have a large group of young people aboard and entertain them with music and dancing and movies, parties of that sort, but her husband when she proposed this would say, "What for? To spoil them?" She told Sanders and Boone: "I find that my style is certainly cramped."[18]

One day there was a presidential trip on the yacht to Hull on Nantucket Bay, and Boone found it exceedingly disagreeable. The seas were stormy, and he worried about the president, who was a woeful sailor and likely to be sick. There also was the mood of John, who was wearing a straw hat his father gave him and did not like it one bit. "I wish to goodness," the Coolidge son said, "it would blow overboard." Mrs. Coolidge and John told the doctor they would like to have a dance at White Court. They raised the question, "What to do with father?"[19]

By the end of July the charms of White Court had worn thin. One day, Boone did not record which, John expressed himself sick of French and would be glad when Saturday came and he could go back to Camp Devens, Massachusetts, where he would be in civilian military training. He bemoaned the fact that he was not able to play tennis, said he "might as well be in the penitentiary as White Court." When he left on August 1, he said he was "damn glad to go."[20]

That year, in October, Mrs. Coolidge asked her husband if he wished to go to Mercersburg for dedication of the school chapel, an impressive Gothic structure designed by the New York architect Ralph Adams Cram (whose other masterful chapel was at Princeton, constructed at about the same time). Coolidge had broken ground for the chapel. His answer was that he would be a fine one to go and talk to the boys when he could not manage his own son.[21]

The next vacation, in 1926, was in the Adirondacks, White Pine Camp near Paul Smiths, New York State, and turned out worse than White Court.[22] A few years later, in her autobiography, Mrs. Coolidge glossed over both of these fiascoes, relating that it was fascinating to go to new places, but such was hardly the case that second year of such experiences. For one thing, her husband did not inquire where she might wish to go for a new experience but foisted it on her. For another, he had the thoughtlessness to take his wife there on July 7, the second anniversary of the death of Calvin Jr.

Like White Court, White Pine Camp seemed to hold attraction. Three miles from a main road, a group of houses made of pine logs, on a bluff overlooking a small lake, it offered fishing, boating, freshwater bathing, paths covered with hemlock bark, rough trails out through the wilderness, tennis available in a court. There was a bowling alley. At Paul Smiths was a hotel, and the president established executive offices in a nearby house.

But the drawbacks were considerable, and Boone disliked the place from the beginning. He and the marine guard established themselves in tents in a camp that overlooked the lake and was removed from the

At White Pine. Courtesy of the Forbes Library, Northampton, Massachusetts.

presidential cabins, which was all right, but tenting held no charms as he had served with the marine brigade in the Second Division during the world war and had seen plenty of tents. The second day at White Pine Camp it rained, and the rain continued for days apparently without end. Swarms of mosquitoes attended the tents and doubled and tripled attendance with the rains. If he turned on a kerosene lamp inside, there were more mosquitoes.

For the president the camp was all right, as he discovered fishing there, and not merely in the lake where he sought bass and pike and could find them even in the rain, but an admirable trout stream was a few miles away, and there he could cast to his heart's content. Every day at the meals in the presidential camp there was a fish entrée, and only twice was it necessary to buy fish in the market. By the end of that summer he was fascinated with fishing, hooked on it he said. The disgusted Boone noticed his fishing procedure or heard of it from the Secret Service agents who accompanied him. The president would throw his line into the bushes on one side of his position, say, on the edge of the lake, and a member of the Secret Service would bait it. He cast the line and without much trouble obtained bites and played the result into shore, whereupon he cast the line and fish to the other side of him, and another Secret Service agent took the fish off the hook, storing it in a bucket or trap. One day, in Boone's presence, Mrs. Coolidge asked her husband to look at his hands, and he showed them to her, pink and clean of fish stains. She discovered that when fishing he wore gloves.

Governor Alfred E. Smith of New York came to White Pine Camp to pay his respects to the president. The governor arrived almost with a crash, bringing his wife, whom he did not often bring to state events, and his son-in-law and daughter, together with a retinue, a troupe, the doctor described them. For a day or two they took over, and among other things dispensed a considerable store of whiskey to the Secret Service agents and reporters, to their private delight. The governor smoked cigars and spoke in a raspy voice and enjoyed every moment of his prominence with the president.

All the while Mrs. Coolidge looked worse and worse, downcast, with little evidence of her usual superabundance of energy, silent when she usually was loquacious. Day after day she spent by herself, for the president went to his office in mornings and fished in afternoons. John was at Devens again, and Boone noticed how lonely she was, hoping to see her son but uncertain whether he might arrive, if the president would ask him to the camp. In bathing one day she confessed her unhappiness. She said she and the president were not at all in accord in regard to John, that her husband did not understand him and made no effort. He reprimanded him, so much that John did not desire to be at home. She did not know if the president would permit John to come to camp. Boone told her he had noticed the dissension and that John needed his mother's guidance into his mature years, to give courage against his father's criticisms and belief that John was lazy, which to Boone's observation, then and through the long years that followed, was impossibly far from the mark.

By mid-August, John arrived, and Boone caught a gleam in his mother's eye as she followed his activities at the camp. The mother wished to be beside him, it seemed, all the time. She feasted on his presence. She could not forbear a criticism that was indirectly of her husband. One day, watching John and Boone play tennis, she scolded him for not retrieving the tennis balls, saying he was much like his father, did not do anything for himself that he could get someone else to do.

For the vacation of 1927 the choice was the Black Hills of South Dakota, the State Game Lodge near, but far enough away from, Rapid City, where the presidential offices were established in the local high school. Coolidge chose the West in 1927 because the country's farmers were unhappy with his refusal to do much about the farm problem, the need somehow to raise the annual incomes of farmers who ever since World War I had been producing too much produce for the national market, with prices falling each year. South Dakota also had good fishing.

Soon after arrival at the lodge he lost his temper with Mrs. Coolidge's Secret Service bodyguard—James Haley, the same who had been scheduled to play doubles with Calvin Jr. when the latter became ill in July 1924. On June 28 Haley took the first lady out for a walk, lost his way, and arrived back at the lodge more than two hours late, to the anger of the president.

The Haley affair, as it became known in the newspaper press, appeared to be entirely the fault of the president but came from the fact that Coolidge had been tense too long and it did not take much to set him off. The details themselves were simple enough. Starling said that Haley, a city boy, had taken his charge out, and when they did not return the president became nervous and sent out search parties. He feared the first lady might have been bitten by a snake; Coolidge was deathly afraid of snakes. The parties found them walking back. By that time the president had lost control of himself, blew up at Haley. On that day Starling was absent, inspecting a fishing place for future reference. Before he could straighten things out, Coolidge sent Haley back to Washington and dismissed him from the White House detail.[23] Word of this got into the newspapers, with much criticism of Coolidge. Mrs. Coolidge was dismayed, although she did not utter a word against her husband's action.

Behind it were the marriage problems, unknown to the newspapers of course. A sensitive man, the first lady's bodyguard had seen her ignored by her husband and sought to cheer her up on walks. This effort on his part may have been noticed by the president, who, Mrs. Coolidge later told Boone, was naturally uneasy about the need for her to be accompanied by a male guard during walks. Even though her husband was president, she said, he was human, even though she was required to have a Secret Service agent in attendance upon her, accompany her whenever she left the White House or, outside Washington, White Court or White Pine Camp or the Game Lodge. Mrs. Coolidge said that Mrs. Stearns fanned the president's feelings of disapproval of Haley by a comment to Coolidge, something about it perhaps being wise for someone other than Haley to accompany her, to ensure that Haley was not doing it all the time.[24]

Haley talked to Boone about how the president ignored the first lady, saying that one time, probably at White Pine Camp, she got a fishhook in a finger and that Coolidge walked off, did not say or do anything, and that he, Haley, had wanted to strike him. Such irritation Haley kept under control, Boone thought.[25]

After the dismissal someone opened a letter from Haley to his wife.[26] It might have been the president himself.

The rest of the time in the Black Hills proved much to the president's satisfaction, which may have helped him concentrate on the political bombshell he announced on August 2. Senator Arthur Capper of Kansas was present at the Game Lodge that morning. Upon arrival

Walking with Secret Service escort, John Fitzgerald, 1928.
Courtesy of the Forbes Library, Northampton, Massachusetts.

at the offices in Rapid City the president was busy. As the news confer-ence approached, the reporters came in and were told that an addi-tional statement would be made at noon. Capper was in an inner office when Coolidge dictated his brief statement to a secretary. That was the first time Capper knew of it. Shortly before noon a typist prepared the required number of statements and cut them into strips for distribu-tion. When the reporters all came in, they received the statement.[27]

As is well known, Capper returned to the lodge for lunch. Meanwhile, the president told the first lady nothing, save that, before he left for Rapid City, he remarked, "I have been president four years today." Upon return shortly after 1:00 P.M. the Coolidges and their guest sat down to lunch. Immediately afterward Coolidge retired for his afternoon nap. His wife sat in the living room with the guest, each in a leather-covered rocking chair.

"Quite a surprise the president gave us this morning," remarked the senator. He looked at Grace Coolidge sharply. "Of course you know all about it."

"I don't believe I do. What was it?" she asked.[28]

The decision of August 2, 1927, made in the Black Hills, not to try for a second presidential nomination in 1928, which because of his national popularity lay virtually open to him, immediately opened the way to the presidency for Secretary of Commerce Hoover. In retrospect the only reason that explains the president's decision to retire is that he at last came to his senses and withdrew. In the Haley affair he realized his incapacity to handle the pressures of the presidency and the marriage.

The remainder of the Coolidge presidency, from the Black Hills statement until departure from Washington on March 4, 1929, was a far better period in family relations, even if it opened with Grace Coolidge's bout with kidney disease. The usual White House round in the autumn of 1927, details of which have appeared earlier, seemed to go without incident, the first lady also appearing at the requisite activities outside the White House. But after the White House reception of February 1, 1928, Mrs. Coolidge collapsed.[29] During the reception Boone watched the president and Mrs. Coolidge shake hands with 3,000 people and saw she was in trouble, was taxing herself, and as soon as the reception was over he hastened upstairs to find her looking perfectly awful. He talked to her in the Lincoln Room and had one of the butlers bring broth and hot coffee. Her pulse was accelerated and weak. She said the president had been tired, and she tried to compensate to make up for his fatigue and apparent disinterest. She had a good night. Boone saw to it that she did, and the next day she told him, "You are a good doctor." That day he treated the president's throat, and Coolidge admitted he had been tired, said that without consulting Coupal or Boone he had taken a large dose of some medicine he thought would quiet him down and had made a mistake. (The president had chosen Major James F. Coupal of the army as his personal physician when he was vice president, and continued him in that role in the presidency; Boone was assistant White House physician even if he, Boone, saw the president and his wife far more frequently than did Coupal.)

The first lady's illness went up and down. February 4, Boone consulted Walter Bloedorn and Paul Dickens, private practitioners in Washington, both internists, and they advised a cystoscopy. But Mrs. Coolidge seemed better. The next day or two matters took a turn for the worse, and Boone advised calling in Hugh Young of Johns Hopkins, who could easily come down from Baltimore. February 8, Boone took the president's wife to the Naval Hospital at Twenty-third and E Streets, driving her in his own car, without Secret Service protection so reporters would not see her leaving the White House, follow them, and produce stories. There Dr. Young examined her, doing the cystoscopy and also taking X-rays, both of which showed an enlarged and misplaced right kidney with obstructed drainage. Young talked with the president, not in the executive offices where the consultation might have been noticed but in the president's study on the White House second floor. He drew a diagram to show the problem. He said the infection could lead to more than local disability but had been diagnosed early, and that while it could lead to long invalidism it could be of a less serious nature.

February 10 saw two serious attacks, very painful. Boone stayed overnight in the White House and brought in a nurse. February 12 he asked Bloedorn to come in and take an electrocardiogram. The consultant was a big, hearty, dignified practitioner, and the Coolidges liked his reassuring presence. The reason for calling in Bloedorn was that Boone's senior, Coupal, thought there might be heart problems.

February 13, Mrs. Coolidge suffered terribly with pain, typical of kidney maladies. The president scarcely left her room.

February 16 was the army and navy reception, a huge, glittering affair, officers in dress uniform, and Mrs. Coolidge's absence was noted. On this occasion Coolidge managed to shake hands with

Portrait of Grace Coolidge, c. 1929. Courtesy of the National First Ladies' Library.

2,360 guests in an hour and five minutes, meaning 1.65 seconds per guest. This was what former president Taft described as pump-handling, and it occasioned a good deal of adverse comment. The president was elated and went upstairs afterward to tell his wife, saying he had made a record, laughing about it.[30]

Early in March, feeling better, the first lady went to Northampton to see her mother, a satisfying trip. Mrs. Goodhue had gone into the hospital in December 1927 and would remain until her death in October 1929. Boone suggested the trip, and Coolidge assented. (This was hardly his response when almost a year before the president's wife suggested a Northampton trip and Coolidge was against it; she had written Therese Hills that all the response she could get was a grunt, "which didn't sound like a sympathetic or an assenting one. No hope!") The trip was almost as good for Mrs. Goodhue as the ministrations of the Northampton doctors. She appeared delighted with her daughter's appearance at the hospital; asked if she was glad to have her near she responded, "Indeed I am!" The entire trip was gratifying, for Boone went along, stayed at 21 Massasoit with Mrs. Coolidge, and ate with the Hillses including Jack and "R.B." or "Daddy," as Mrs. Coolidge described him. Another trip proved necessary a few weeks later, but the initial one did wonders for the first lady's morale.[31]

For some weeks everything seemed all right, and then early in the summer there was more kidney trouble. It threatened to get in the way of a summer vacation planned for a small island in the Brule River near Superior, Wisconsin. Coolidge had decided on the Brule because he could fish in the river and nearby streams. He had become exhilarated by the prospect of fishing beginning with the vacation in the Adirondacks. The new attack also threatened to get in the way of what he considered an absolute necessity, which was to get out of Washington before the Republican National Convention opened in Kansas City. He was not enthused by Secretary of Commerce Hoover's presidential candidacy and did not wish to be at hand in the capital, where reporters could ask him what he thought about Hoover as a candidate.

The early summer kidney attack subsided, proving the last visitation of the painful malady, and the Coolidges got out of the capital for the vacation and ahead of the convention and reporters.

About this time everything straightened out over the president's inability to handle his son John, for the latter was getting special handling from Florence Trumbull. After the 1926 vacation in the Adirondacks the president had sent Starling up to Amherst to room with him and presumably keep him studying and generally in

Therese Hills, Grace's Northampton friend.
Courtesy of the Forbes Library, Northampton, Massachusetts.

order. Friendship with Florence made that unnecessary, although the presidential harassment continued for a while and caused an occasional flare-up. Starling returned to Washington at the end of 1926. For a while John felt it necessary to send his father his expenses—or else his father demanded them. One rundown showed

$1 for church, $.50 for Listerine, $1.55 for writing paper, $.50 for a haircut. Another showed $1 for Sunday night supper, carfare to Northampton and back $.56. On another John wrote to his father, "That one dollar and fifty cents was to have a suit dry cleaned, not pressed." Once he needed a check; he was not allowed to keep a checking account. He said he needed the check for board, which was $9.[32] June 11, 1927, four days before the president and Mrs. Coolidge left for their third summer vacation, in the Black Hills, John's father wrote the following:

> Your letter has been received and check is enclosed. When you left here last spring I understood that you were to be met at Hartford and go at once to the Governor's house. The newspapers reported that instead of that you went to a night club, and that you did not go to church the next day. This did not make a very good picture. When you are visiting at one place and Sunday comes you should go to church whether the people where you happen to be stopping wish to go or not. It will not do any harm for you to set them a good example.

John was so irritated by all this that the next year, when his mother was visiting his grandmother in Northampton, he told his mother he did not see how she could put up with his father.[33]

In 1928 the president allowed a national fund-raising for Clarke School, a sign that everything was loosening, even if his son John saw continuing tension. Admittedly the idea of raising $2 million for the school was not that of the president or his wife but of the New York financial publisher, owner of the *Wall Street Journal*, Clarence Barron, who raised the possibility and whose participation alone, with all the large donors he could bring in, ensured its success. The president stipulated that the Coolidge Fund would not in any way give appearance of pressure from the retiring administration upon contributors. The purpose was to develop an international reputation for Clarke's teaching of deaf children, a teacher training program connected with Smith College, where the president, William Nielsen, was one of Clarke's trustees, and to expand the school's research department to include social and psychological aspects of deafness, vocational guidance, and preschool education for deaf children. Large contributors included William Boyce

Florida, January 24, 1930.
Courtesy of the Forbes Library, Northampton, Massachusetts.

Thompson and family, $135,000; Earle P. Charlton of Fall River, who was the national chairman; Henry L. Doherty and Fred M. Kirby, $110,000 each; Andrew Mellon, $100,000; and Cyrus H. Curtis, Edward S. Harkness, William A. Paine, Frank Phillips, and John J. Raskob, $50,000 each. The national chairman announced the fund's virtual completion on March 4, 1929. On March 12 the Coolidges together with Clarke officials, townspeople, and schoolchildren crowded into Gardiner Greene Hubbard Chapel, and there Mrs. Coolidge handed over the fund results, oversubscribed from the $2 million goal, to the school's retired principal, Caroline Yale, aged eighty, in a wheelchair, who accepted them for the school, with which she had been associated for fifty-nine of the sixty-one years of Clarke's existence.[34]

After Wisconsin, the summer of 1928, there followed a series of delightful if smaller vacations. The first was to the Swannanoa Country Club in the Blue Hills of Virginia, and on Thanksgiving Day the president and first lady motored to Charlottesville, lunched with the president of the university, and saw the first quarter of a football game between Virginia and the University of North Carolina. For Christmas they journeyed to Sapelo Island on the Georgia coast, a wonderful place. There the artist Frank A. Salisbury did individual portraits of the president and Mrs. Coolidge. The president went out turkey hunting, for which he had practiced skeet shooting on the Brule, and the take was minuscule, actually zero, but enjoyable. Mrs. Coolidge relaxed on the sea island with its half-tropical scenery.

In February 1929, they took advantage of a request by the philanthropist Edward W. Bok that they travel to Mountain Lake, Florida, to dedicate the bird sanctuary and singing tower that Bok had arranged. Why on earth such a place was necessary was a mystery that only the philanthropist knew, but it was convenient for the presidential couple. Bok probably did not know that the president privately described the establishment as an effort to teach the birds to sing.

Not long after the Florida trip it was time to leave the White House. Mrs. Coolidge visited the wardroom of the *Mayflower* for a farewell and refreshments and came with a little iron Scottie doorstop, which she left. At that time the stands along Pennsylvania Avenue were going up, everything in near readiness for the inauguration. To the Scottie she attached a poem of her own composition, expressive of her mood as her husband's long years in Washington were coming to an end:

> Hark, hark, the dogs do bark.
> The Hoovers are coming to town.
> The Coolidges depart
> With a pain in the heart
> And Congress looks on with a frown.
>
> The City is dressed with its beautiful best.
> The Avenue bristles with seats.
> The *Mayflower* rocks
> At the Navy Yard docks
> While we laugh and partake of the eats.
> "Only," a dog.[35]

CHAPTER 6

TOGETHER, ALONE

The first dozen years after Grace Coolidge returned to Northampton were a strange time in her life. Her husband, the former president, died on January 5, 1933, suddenly, of a heart attack, and the shock was extremely difficult. His presence had formed her life, much more than she realized. It had not been an easy marriage. The two had always made room for each other, and yet her husband's political career defined what she could or could not do. Initially, in Northampton with the boys, she enjoyed a considerable freedom. The vice presidency and the presidency not so; she had her public duties. In the early part of her marriage she determined to get along, and she kept to that rule, even when in 1924–1927 it became exceedingly difficult. The return to Northampton made the marriage much easier. Then he was gone.

After her husband passed on, there necessarily was a change of direction, so to speak. At first she was confused. Her biographer, Ishbel Ross, found a letter to a friend that, with exaggeration, described her plight: "I am just a lost soul. Nobody is going to believe how I miss being told what to do. My father always told me what I had to do. Then Calvin told me what I had to do."[1] But then the change took place, and it was drastic. She became fast friends with a liberated woman, Florence Bannard ("Florie") Adams. Mrs. Adams was a Smith College graduate (1905) who later took an M.A. in history

(1930). She was a divorcée who lived at 16 Massasoit Street and, as Grace Coolidge once said, would do anything. An early outcome of their friendship was a series of trips to North Carolina beginning in April 1933 and a trip to Europe in 1936 that lasted six months. In 1931, Mrs. Coolidge had ventured the latter proposition to her husband, for Therese Hills proposed it, and he harrumphed and told her it might derange American foreign policy—this was the year of the Hoover moratorium on international payment of war debts and reparations, the debts owed largely to the United States, which gave economic breathing room to the hard-pressed republic in Germany that had established itself after collapse of the German Empire in 1918. Grace was surprisingly irritated, and open about her irritation, for she wrote Hillsy that she had to remain at home "unoffensively." She added, "Blah!!!"[2] In 1936 when she and Florie went to Europe no one could stop her. The trip was altogether enjoyable, and Florie drove her big automobile from one scenic place to another, and if necessary during their travels the two women roughed it in ways unconventional for a former first lady. Grace often wore trousers, which would have enraged her husband. Upon return from Europe she frequently was gone from Northampton, to a mountain in North Carolina. It was the last mountain on the Blue Ridge chain, 3,000 feet above sea level. Florie owned a part of it. Grace Coolidge and Florie trudged up and down, picnicked on the way, and, as the former first lady described her new life, had "great fun." Her husband would have hated it. Life with Florie Adams began to resemble a rebellion from the limits imposed upon her since 1905—the limits of her father before that had never amounted to much. On December 7, 1941, all this came to an end.

When the Coolidges waved good-bye to a throng of admirers in Washington's Union Station on March 4, 1929, and returned to Northampton, it was a marked change of scene, not quite as much as for Grace in the mid-1930s but comparatively a change. Their special car arrived in beloved Northampton early in the morning, and after arising and having breakfast they set out by automobile for 21 Massasoit Street. All the way out the curbs were lined with well-wishers from the hometown, including hundreds of Smith College girls, the latter not altogether dressed as they wore curlers and scarves to hide them. Everyone waved.

Mrs. Reckahn was on hand in the kitchen, and it seemed as if only a month or two had elapsed since 1921. The old routine set in. The retired president accepted the offer of his law partner, Mr. Hemenway (as the partner always was known to the senior partner), to take his front office on the second floor of the unadorned building just off Main Street, on which the firm's name, Coolidge and Hemenway, was duly marked (and would remain marked for decades thereafter). Coolidge went to the office every morning and there sat in a plain chair with his feet in the wastebasket and dictated letters to a multitude of correspondents. It was tedious work, even with his customary short answers, for there were so many letters. Most of them desired him to make speeches, and he declined them, one after another; he was not through with speeches, but they were not his intention of retirement for they required so much care and time.[3]

Not long afterward, in January 1930, the former president and his wife took refuge in travel, to which they had become accustomed during the White House years. They undertook—somewhat to Grace Coolidge's surprise—another trip to Florida, six weeks in the Lakeside Inn at Mount Dora, and followed with a visit to New Orleans and thence to California. In Florida they enjoyed the change of climate and scenery. In New Orleans the former president and his wife saw the sights, without undue appreciation.

In California the notable activity was a visit to San Simeon, the castle of the newspaper publisher William Randolph Hearst, which amused both the head of the Coolidge family and his wife. The magnificence of the place caught their imagination. Grace Coolidge told the castle's owner that all the place lacked was an organ. He demurred, relating that an organ would be out of place, for it belonged in a cathedral. "Very good," said Mrs. Coolidge, as she reported her words to the robins, "bring over a cathedral."[4] Not so good, if momentary, was the experience at San Simeon of being stuck in an elevator. The former first lady and her husband had the choice of walking up circling stone steps to the Doric suite on the third floor across the front of the castle or taking the Otis elevator, hidden away in the center of a huge circular column. She chose the elevator, and when descending to lunch one day, before her husband was ready, it stuck between floors. She had her knitting, but the elevator was small and there was no place to sit, no room for a seat. There was plenty of

Calvin and Grace share a porch and a chuckle, c. 1930.
Courtesy of the Clarke School for the Deaf.

light, but the little cage was chilly and apparently had no chance of attracting attention. The elevator had an alarm gong, but the power was off. Workers on the roof were chiseling stone and unable to hear. She tried yodeling, and after a performance—she said there were many—and half an hour of knitting she heard a voice from above inquiring, "Somebody call?" The man summoned an electrician, and after sounds of tapping, creaking, and several jerkings the box finally moved and she reached the lower level as the guests were assembling for lunch.[5]

At the castle the proprietor showed movies every night, being himself the owner of a studio and sponsor of the actress Marion Davies, who lived at the castle but did not make an appearance during the residence of the Coolidges. Grace Coolidge had only to mention the name of a film of interest and as if by magic it would appear on the evening screen program.

Hearst treated his guests to drinks, and according to a biographer of the press magnate, whose story may not be accurate, the following colloquy occurred between Hearst and Calvin Coolidge after the former president told his host that he did not drink.

"Neither do I," Hearst nodded, "but I find that a sip of this wine is an excellent appetizer."

"Is it alcoholic?" Coolidge inquired.

"Not perceptibly. The alcoholic content is slight."

Calvin Coolidge took a glass of Tokay, tried it, and his eyes brightened. He had another. "I must remember this," he said.[6]

In California the Coolidges spent a day in Hollywood, watching the cameras photograph extras in several productions, meeting Douglas Fairbanks and his wife, Mary Pickford, together with producers and heads of studios. At the outset they were inducted into a breakfast club where the former president declined to speak, Mrs. Coolidge confining herself to two words, one of which was "hello."

In February 1931, Mrs. Coolidge, her friend Mrs. Hills, and her new daughter-in-law (married in 1929), the former Florence Trumbull, journeyed to Newport News to christen the new Dollar Steamship Company's liner, *President Coolidge.* Together with its sister ship, the *President Hoover,* it was the largest liner ever built in the United States, weighing 23,000 tons. The wife of the former president christened it with a bottle of water from the Black River at Plymouth Notch. During World War II the ship was taken over by the navy as a transport and was sunk by an American mine in the New Hebrides in 1942, with loss of 4 men out of the 4,000 aboard.

Not long after return to Northampton the former president finished his autobiography, which sold for a high price in the national book market of the time, three dollars. His wife made an arrangement with local bookstores that for an extra dollar he would autograph a book, the money going to the missionary fund of the Edwards Church.

In an account of Grace Coolidge it is perhaps allowable to remark the qualities of her husband's autobiography, although much has been written about it. The book was a moneymaker. Coolidge's estate of $700,000 was not in principal due to the autobiography, but it did bring in $5 per word, including the articles *a* and *the,* as critics pointed out. At a time when a day's hard work by a laborer might have brought half as much, especially as the Depression that began in 1929 deepened into crisis in 1933, this was big money. But the book revealed the former president's poetic inner nature. It offered memorable details of life in Plymouth Notch that formed his early years, including the tragedy of his mother, her death at such an early age, and that of his sister Abbie, whose young life, cut short, promised so much. The book showed how the thin young boy from the Notch learned that life was serious, as in the Notch it had to be—what it was like to grow up in the silences of that lonely little place up the gorge from Plymouth Union, "nestled" (the hackneyed word was appropriate) on a sort of plateau that looked out on the rolling Green Mountains where naught could be heard but cowbells and crows and sometimes the hooting of a lovesick bear, the silence saying what Coolidge later told the Massachusetts General Assembly, "Do the day's work." A reader can see why Grace Coolidge wrote, "Life was always a serious matter with him. He never felt the need of play—wouldn't have known how to satisfy the need if he had recognized it. Early in our acquaintance I tried to teach him and sometimes he made an effort to respond but usually tried to show me how important it was to face life in serious mien."[7]

In addition to the autobiography there was a daily newspaper column, "Calvin Coolidge Says," which lasted a year, July 1, 1930 through June 1931. Its author terminated it because the pressure of its deadline (he never was late) was too much. Like the autobiography it was a moneymaker, at $3.25 a word, $643.50 a column of 198 words. It brought the syndicator $203,045, a substantial part of which went to Coolidge. Widely read, it never was critical of the Hoover administration and confined its advice to what critics said were bromides, but taken as a distillation of the wisdom of the Notch they made sense.

In retirement the house at Massasoit Street did not work, for the tourists made life difficult, and something had to be done, which was to move to another house. There was a constant purr in the street from their cars as they slowly drove by. They stopped and voices asked, "Where is he?" and if Coolidge was sitting on the porch holding Rob Roy and the chow Tiny Tim by a rope, a voice would say, "There he is!" Even the children on Massasoit Street misbehaved, knowing their parents' former neighbor had been famous and was now back in the double house at Number 21. The present writer once met a retired psychologist who related that he grew up on Massasoit and one day went down to the Coolidge house and rapped on the window, and when the former president looked out, the boy spat on the window and ran away. His mother made him go back and apologize. It was too much, and Coolidge bought The Beeches, which had a gate and nine acres of ground sloping toward the Connecticut River. The cost was $36,000. His wife told a friend that reports of its spaciousness, an estate it was called, were exaggerated, although she admitted it was a change from Massasoit.[8] It had been built in 1914–1915 by Henry Noble McCracken, an English professor at Smith College, who became president of Vassar College, and thereafter the house was owned for twelve years by Mr. and Mrs. Morris L. Comey. He died and she decided to go to New York. The newspapers made too much of the size of the house, she told Joel Boone. The Coolidges could count only eleven of the sixteen rooms. One was a billiard room on the third floor, which they used as storage. The "electric" elevator was a push-pull lift, for freight, although Mrs. Reckahn could get in it and ride if she knew the system. There were two guest rooms with baths, to put up John and Florence and friends, and a sunroom and two sleeping porches. It had a tennis court enclosed by a wire fence on which were ramblers and suchlike. A terrace ran down to the meadow below, paths and steps cut in and edged with logs. Wild flowers grew along the banks, and there were a vegetable garden and fruit trees.[9]

The Beeches had its usefulness, but the former first lady was not excited by it and hated to leave Number 21, the house of so many memories. It was another temporary house. Her husband had bought it, not her. It had been available, and he showed no interest and then bought it. "No one ever knows what plans are taking shape in his mind," she wrote carefully to Grace Medinus, "until he is ready for action."[10]

Having made this purchase, Coolidge turned to another house project, a new house at the Notch that would be an appendage to the old. He described it to his wife as a lean-to. The house of his father had not been impossible, for his father and mother-in-law lived happily in it and Victoria Coolidge spent time there, an evidence of which was the front bay window constructed for her. Calvin and Grace Coolidge maintained it after Colonel Coolidge's death in 1926, but it had few facilities for heat—none for heat upstairs—and plumbing was outdoors. Lighting was still kerosene. To solve all this Coolidge conceived of the lean-to, which years afterward would be removed to another location on the farm but for the moment was entirely satisfactory. Grace described the house to Ivah Gale. Across the front was a long living room, paneled on the window side and with floor-to-ceiling bookshelves on the other three sides. A large brick fireplace stood next to the door. Back of this were bedrooms and a bath and linen closet. A screened porch, leading from Mrs. Coolidge's bedroom, was good for summer sleeping. Upstairs were two guest bedrooms, a room for her husband's secretary and a bath, and a large linen closet.[11] The house was the former president's project, and his wife carefully let him handle it. As she put it to John's mother-in-law, Maude Trumbull, the wing was his "and I am letting him flap it."[12]

At the Notch the domestic help situation needed reinforcement when the Coolidges and possibly guests were in residence. The aging housekeeper Aurora Pierce was there, and they brought up help from The Beeches, at first a member of the Christian Science Church who could not get along with her helper. The helper went to cook for a boardinghouse, and they employed another Christian Scientist and matters settled down.[13]

The Notch in summertime held many attractions, and Grace Coolidge, in the past an occasional visitor, was growing attached to them. In September 1931, she wrote Hillsy in Northampton that she really was enjoying herself. She was becoming a hayseed and suspected she would return with a nasal drawl akin to her husband's. Tourists were diminishing, although a frost meant they would increase because of the turning of the leaves. She was living in the old house, but the new one was rapidly being completed, and her husband was getting over there at 7:00 to supervise the workmen.

It really is lovely up here and I have stayed long enough to grow accustomed to the independence and time to make the most of the living. This morning, there was a heavy white frost on the meadows and in the moonlight it was as though someone had taken a brush, dipped it in silver and painted the scene. Then this morning, when the early sun shone on it it seemed that it was being brought to actuality. A fire in the sitting room stove keeps us snug and warm. The coals keep over night so that when Elizabeth comes down in the morning, along about six o'clock, she puts in a few shavings, some old shingle and then some wood and all is warm and comfortable in fifteen or twenty minutes.[14]

The wedding anniversaries passed. In 1929 a *New York Times* reporter came up to Northampton to see the dogs and said she had asked Coolidge at the office about the anniversary. He replied that he and his wife never planned anything in particular and preferred to celebrate every day.[15] The next year Grace noticed there was a sort of celebration, but it was incidental to their going to Boston for the American Legion convention. Rather than motor far on Sunday they stopped at the Wayside Inn. Her husband had been there on his way to the Republican state convention and liked the cottage cheese. The inn closed to guests on Sundays but took in the Coolidges by arrangement. They occupied the private suite of Henry and Mrs. Ford. The kitchen help cooked Sunday dinner in the old-fashioned way, in an old fireplace. The roast was baked in a Dutch oven, the vegetables in iron pots on the crane, hoecake in the ashes, and Indian pudding and pumpkin pie in the brick oven. They ate at the old tavern table in front of the fire with everything dished up in their presence. "Another adventure into dreamland."[16]

The Coolidges went to Plymouth Notch for the last time in June 1932, and Grace Coolidge may have had a presentiment of what was to come. She wrote Ivah that after arrival her husband was in bed for a week. "The presidency is a wearing job and takes its toll from any man who serves therein. Calvin never was set up as ruggedly as some and there are times when I feel that those years took most of the reserve."[17] He summoned the children, John and Florence. A postcard of August 1, 1932, quoted "father," who said, "I should think the children had better spend their vacation here this summer." He offered the suggestion under the excuse that if they went to Maine, as they had planned, it would cost too much—the year was near the trough of the Great Depression and money hard to come by.[18] That summer on the Coolidges' twenty-seventh anniversary he was working on his last speech, which President Hoover begged him to make in the campaign that was faltering against the popularity of the Democratic candidate, Governor Franklin D. Roosevelt of New York. Hoover sent Postmaster General Harry S. New, the former Indiana senator, up to the Notch and the two met on the road, one limousine going up to the Notch, the other going the other way and containing the former president. Coolidge stopped, and New's driver backed down. "Seen ya" was the greeting, after which he agreed to the speech.[19]

The anniversary that summer was described by Coolidge's wife in a touching letter to Grace Medinus:

> And so, dear G. G., if you listen in, next Tuesday evening, be not overcritical and remember that much life blood has been drawn for "the cause." Thus, you see, a mere wedding anniversary did not enter largely into the scheme of things as they were, yesterday. Indeed, I think it would have been overlooked entirely had it not been for some congratulatory messages received at the other desk. I was writing away industriously at mine when the morning mail came in. Presently, I heard footsteps crossing the parlor, descending the two steps into the living room where my desk (Sarah Brewer Coolidge's desk) sits by the first window at the left. A pause—I see feet standing just under my right elbow—a voice, "Mommy, do you know what day this is?" "Yes." "What day is it?" "Our wedding anniversary, twenty-seventh." "Why didn't you tell me?" "I thought you had enough on your mind." "Well, I wanted to know about it." Then a little kiss down under my ear somewhere and retreating footsteps, closed doors in the sitting room and low murmur of dictation.[20]

On the last day of that year he wrote to Ted Clark that he felt worn out, that he knew his work was done. A friend called at The Beeches on New Year's Day, and he said he was very comfortable because he was not doing anything of any account. "I'm afraid I'm all burned out. But I'm very comfortable." A few days later his wife went downtown to market and returned to find him on the upstairs bedroom floor. In faraway Washington, Colonel Starling read the news that evening. The following morning he took the train to Northampton and came into the house, where he met Ted Clark and Mr. Stearns. He said he came as a friend, not an emissary from Washington. Mrs. Coolidge heard him talking and called downstairs, "Don't I hear Colonel Starling's voice?" Clark answered her, saying Starling had just arrived. "Please tell him to come upstairs," she said. She met him with arms outstretched, put her head on his shoulders, and wept.[21]

After the funeral in the Edwards Church and the addition of another Coolidge headstone in the cemetery in the Notch, the life of Grace Coolidge changed dramatically. She was of course no longer together, in what in the horse age was known as double harness; she was alone with her memories of the great times in which her husband had taken part, and she too had taken part. But the president's death allowed a freedom she could only imagine during the years together.

Grace Coolidge possessed much of the stern stuff that had driven her husband—she had to have it to live with him so long. She recognized his idealism when she met him, and liked it, for she shared it—life was serious. Her husband, she knew, had an elfish side, which he allowed himself to show on some occasions, but not many. Starling, who saw so much of him, recognized it and defined his presidential walking partner and fishing partner as half owl, half elf. The elf was visible in the quiet remarks, what became known as Coolidge stories. Some were visible only to Starling and Mrs. Coolidge—about Edward Bok endowing the tower in Florida to teach the birds to sing. There was the story about the preacher and sin, not of the genre, and the serious one about why the European nations owing war debts to the United States should pay them rather than default on them ("They hired the money, didn't they?"), which may have been part of it, as Mrs. Coolidge once told the present writer. For the most part the president could not enjoy life, and that made it impossible for his wife to enjoy life, beyond moments and snatches when small opportunities became available or almost forced themselves upon both of them.

With Calvin Coolidge's passing the repression of all the years was gone, and Grace Coolidge opened up, became a different person because the half of her being that had been kept under wraps was able to appear, to emerge. She did things she had wished to do and could not. Perhaps it was a return to her years in Burlington when she and her friends took the *Vermont II* and journeyed across Lake Champlain to the rocks and vistas and sometimes old fortifications that surrounded the town on the Green Mountain side of the lake, across from the Adirondacks.

The change became evident upon better acquaintance with a longtime neighbor on Massasoit Street, Mrs. Adams. The latter was something else. Mrs. Adams enjoyed life. She had not enjoyed the presence of her husband and dropped him somewhere in the past. The marriage resulted in a daughter, Janey, who was like her mother, drawn to her own pursuits, and sometime after Mrs. Coolidge joined forces with Mrs. Adams in trips to North Carolina and in 1936 the trip to Europe, Janey married and presented her husband with two children and then, taking a leaf from her mother, dropped him to pursue her interest in studying musicology at Smith and in London. Janey moved in and out of Grace Coolidge's companionship with Mrs. Adams. The movements, like those of Florie, were memorable. One time when Janey's children were growing up the boy appeared to have swallowed thumbtacks. His sister told Janey, who looked in his mouth and found two. Hospital X-rays showed the youngster to be tackless.

Florie Adams was altogether unlike the far more sedate Therese Hills, and Grace Coolidge recognized that fact, also that in the early 1930s Hillsy became less interesting. Her husband failed to take care of himself. Mrs. Coolidge told Boone, who knew him, that he suffered colds, abominable (she misspelled it and it may have been abdominal) ones, two in three weeks. He thought and talked too much about himself. He indulged in rich foods. Because of the colds he kept his weight down, and pointed with pride to this rather unusual way of weight loss. He kept Hillsy's spirits down, which was "the worst feature of a bad business." There also was Mrs. Hills's preoccupation with what was happening to her church in Northampton, which was the Episcopal church. Mrs. Coolidge did not take this seriously, perhaps saying to herself the old description of Episcopal spirituality, low and lazy, broad and hazy, high and crazy. Hillsy could not lean on her church because the rector was calling himself a priest and moving the liturgy upward. "I try to laugh her out of it and tell her it doesn't matter whether it is high or low" and she could "still worship the Lord," but the point was lost.[22]

Jack Hills, like other boys, had grown up, and that tie no longer held, what with John Coolidge married and in Connecticut.

Florie Adams was different, which suited Mrs. Coolidge. Hillsy did not understand it and wrote to Boone, "For over twenty years—

I have seen her every day and it is a bit hard getting adjusted to this new way."[23] The former first lady, however, liked it. Boone would not have thought it, but Florie was what the doctor ordered.

At first the two women got out together. In April 1933 they went to North Carolina near Tryon, where Florie owned part of the top of the mountain, having inherited it from an uncle. Thereafter their principal occupation was going south to the mountain, where they stayed for months. It was 950 miles from Northampton to Tryon, in a time of no interstates and two-lane state and national roads (the latter had been organized in 1925 during the Coolidge administration) that passed through the worst concentrations of stoplights and main streets in all villages, towns, and metropolises. Anyone who has not driven in the pre-1960s era will not understand what traffic in the 1930s was. Mrs. Adams, undaunted, rushed down to Tryon each time in three days, perhaps with Mrs. Coolidge holding on for dear life. Once there they did everything in what Grace before 1933 might have pronounced excess, but when she did it with Florie she enjoyed every minute of the experience. The two walked down the mountain, a long walk, and up the mountain, for what might have been twelve miles, Grace told John. She admitted it was a pull coming up. Once in place, at the top, the two played rummy, and Grace wrote that they had played, "thus far," seventy-two games, score even.[24]

In April 1934, when they had been back and forth for a year, Grace and Florie heard the rumor that started somewhere or other that Mrs. Coolidge was going to marry her husband's former secretary, the Indiana congressman Everett Sanders, whose wife had died. According to the rumor, Sanders and the former Mrs. Coolidge would live on the several-hundred-acre Maryland estate of the wealthy Sanders. The rumor caught attention of reporters, and Mrs. Coolidge had some fun with it. She wrote John, who may have wondered, "Here she is, safe and sound and single, and in so far as she is aware, in her right mind." Someone, she said, went crazy, but she was not the one. She followed with an explanation of how she and Florie and two cousins of the latter were on a picnic and heard a motor, and it was a driver and someone in the back. The driver asked where Mrs. Adams lived, and the group learned that the person in back was a reporter. Florie told them Mrs. Coolidge was not there and arranged for the reporter to come to the house the next day. This was a reporter with Associated Press and United Press connections, and the rumor had grown to where Mrs. Coolidge was on her honeymoon. Next day the reporter arrived, and Florie told her—she and Grace must have talked over the answer the night before—that she personally could deny the rumor. Two years later, Sanders married, but not to Mrs. Coolidge. "So," she added in another letter to John, "Mr. Sanders has married his nurse! Her picture doesn't fill me with enthusiasm but I know what newspaper pictures are. Anyhow, I am glad he has found somebody to his liking."[25]

In December 1934, the two made a trip to Tryon during which they passed through Washington, an adventure in itself. In the capital, which Mrs. Coolidge had not seen since 1929, she toured the sights. She wore her horn-rimmed glasses, and no one recognized her except a policeman outside the National Museum, who at one time was attached to the marines on the *Mayflower*. She swore him to secrecy. "He was so pleased that I was almost glad that he knew me." They visited the Shakespeare library, the Folger, and went to the Smithsonian to see the gowns of presidents' wives. They had lunch at the Allies' Inn. They drove around to see the new departmental buildings on or near Pennsylvania Avenue erected by the Roosevelt administration to bring together the scattered offices of cabinet departments, each new building of a gigantic classical design, at once impractical and cavernous and expensive so as to give employment in the depths of the Depression.

In the spring of 1935, Mrs. Coolidge moved out of The Beeches, dark and filled with memory of finding her husband dead, and joined the household of Mrs. Adams. She kept The Beeches for a while, to be sure she enjoyed living with Florie and with Janey, who was staying there while taking a year of work at Smith. The third member of the household was Florence Snow, alumnae secretary at the college, who had lived with Florie for ten years. There Grace Coolidge could enjoy the family life she had known since entering the tightly knit little group in Burlington, now with Grace the only survivor. She possessed her own, with Calvin and John and Calvin II, as she sometimes described the tall, thin boy who left in 1924. With Mrs. Adams's ménage she could enjoy the life missed since the passing of her husband, impossible at The Beeches alone.

About this time there was a change in the appearance of Mrs. Coolidge. The *New York Times* and *Washington Post* announced it early in May 1935, for reporters ascertained that the former first lady had taken a step already made by many American women. A few years before, in 1931, a *Post* writer had declared that Grace Coolidge had bobbed her hair. The writer clearly was uncertain, hedging her story and giving as her proof anonymous Vermonters near Plymouth. Little more of the issue was heard until 1935, when reports became certain. According to the *Post* on May 6, she made the change. It was the third such move by leading American women. The first had been the decision of the dancer Irene Castle, who took the step at the beginning of the war. Some years later America's sweetheart, Mary Pickford, followed, and was in tears as her golden tresses fell to the barbershop floor, but explained that it symbolized her decision no longer to accept roles of little girls; she would play adult roles. Unfortunately, observed the *Post*, the result was the biblical experience of Samson; she lost her appeal to adult audiences. The *Post* did not offer the reasoning behind Mrs. Coolidge's decision, which may have been the impulsiveness of Florie Adams. In any event it did not matter, both newspapers agreed, for Mrs. Coolidge always was perfectly groomed.

Once Mrs. Coolidge was living in Mrs. Adams's small group, she and Florie began planning the European trip. This was a far more venturesome proposition in the 1920s and 1930s than later, and while many Americans visited Europe and had done so for decades, a trip was expensive then and out of the ordinary. For the two it was entirely possible because both were well-off. Grace Coolidge was not a millionaire but had more money to spend, properly to be sure, than she could spend in Northampton.

The planning stage was expansive and early in 1936 passed into reality. Off went the adventuresome women, Grace and Florie. They traveled in ten countries in a convertible Auburn automobile that they named "Oliver," and must have been a sight as they passed through farming and other country and through the streets of medieval towns or large cities with streets tracing older times and architecture. Mrs. Coolidge's hair would be bobbed, she would have worn her trousers, and might have been smoking a cigarette, as she had done for years but never in public.[26] She perhaps disguised herself with the glasses she wore in Washington two years earlier.

It is of interest that Grace Coolidge went to Europe in the year of the most important international crisis in the 1930s, until the German attack on Poland in 1939, namely, the occupation of the Rhineland by Germany under its führer, Adolf Hitler. Elected chancellor in 1933, Hitler proclaimed himself führer, or leader, of the Third Reich, the Third Empire of Germany in succession to the second that ended in 1918 (the first was the Holy Roman Empire of medieval times). He broke the Treaty of Versailles in 1934 when he signed a naval agreement with Great Britain contrary to the disarmament clauses of the treaty of 1919. In 1936, when German troops marched into the Rhineland, forbidden to them by Versailles, he did more than simple treaty breaking; he separated France from its eastern allies, notably Czechoslovakia, opening the way for World War II. The führer prepared to remove the troops if the British and French governments threatened force, but he got away with it. From then on it was only a matter of time before he started taking apart the weak governments of eastern Europe beginning with Austria in 1938.

The Rhineland crisis, the result a German diplomatic victory because of the timidity of the British and French governments, their desire for peace at any price, "peace in our time," to use the description of Prime Minister Neville Chamberlain in 1938 after return from Munich, was far more important than negotiation of the Hoover moratorium in 1931 that for a short time consumed the diplomacy of the West and concerned former president Coolidge. In 1938, Mrs. Coolidge wrote Boone, then in San Diego aboard the navy hospital ship USS *Rescue,* sensing for the first time what she and Mrs. Adams had done. She remarked what a mess Europe was in, wrote of Boone's new assignment of responsibility for establishing a medical department for the First Marine Force, and said it gave her "an awful turn."[27]

February 18, 1936, the grand tour began. Mrs. Coolidge wrote John and Florence and their daughter Cynthia, who arrived in 1934, every week, on Sundays, addressing them as "Dear Children" and signing herself "Mother." She wrote once in a while to Ivah and to the robins when the bird flew in, not an easy flight. The letters bear witness to the infinite detail by which Grace's friend Florie, who had been to Europe many times, conducted the tour.[28]

The first stop was England and Scotland. When the *Bremen* approached Southampton but did not dock, two friends came out on the tender to meet them, a professor at Smith, Mary Ellen Chase, and a woman who was studying at Cambridge, with whom Miss Chase was living. Oliver, the car, was hauled up by a crane and placed on the deck of a small transport. A customs officer came out on the tender and got them through inspection of their luggage, no problem for Mrs. Coolidge, who had a diplomatic passport and letters from all the ambassadors of the countries they proposed to visit. Florie probably went through customs with an extra push. The two drove to London and started the British phase of the tour, staying in the American Women's Club for two weeks. From there they made a sort of circle, up to Edinburgh and back through the cathedral towns. Along the way they saw the house of Harold Nicolson, who had done a biography of Dwight Morrow, who died in 1931, and saw the garden of Nicolson's wife, the writer Virginia Sackville-West. On the way to Cambridge they stopped at Abbottsford, the house of Sir Walter Scott. One can see the two tourists as they virtually invited themselves in. They saw a wooden door through a fence and went in, even though the house was closed, and saw a man coming down the path and asked when the house was open. He hesitated and then took them in, and they saw everything, including the bed where Sir Walter Scott died.

Passing across the Channel as soon as the Rhineland crisis seemed to settle down, they proceeded from Belgium to southern France and there employed an early version of the hub system, copied by American airlines, taking tours from such places as Angers. They went to Limoges, through lovely country, and saw the prehistoric caves of the Cro-Magnon era. Carcassone was another hub, thence Toulouse, apple trees in bloom and spring flowers, great stretches of yellow mustard, gorgeous days, nights a fine moon.

In Spain it was Barcelona and the Balearic Isles.

They did not go to Greece, although they considered it. They thought they could squeeze it in, but time did not permit.

Nor did they go to Italy. They went to Menton and looked into Italy but did not venture. The Italian lakes beckoned, but Mussolini's ambitions in Ethiopia—his troops entered Addis Ababa—made them impossible, and "we decided he could keep his old Italy. He would undoubtedly be filled with remorse if he knew about it."

They motored through the Swiss Alps in a thrilling experience, went over the Simplon Pass the first day it opened, "and it wasn't too open at that." They had near encounters but nothing serious and followed a heavy thunderstorm into Lugano in high spirits. Next morning they found a message from the garage telling them the car had two flat front tires; somewhere Oliver picked up large numbers of small tacks that worked into the tires.

Every place was an adventure. In Marseilles, Florie wished Grace to have bouillabaisse, made to perfection, she said, with a kind of fish available only in that part of the Mediterranean and untransportable. Grace ate it and was not ready for an encore.

Switzerland was probably the favorite country, and if Mrs. Coolidge had decided to stay in Europe, she might have taken up residence in Lucerne. She lost her heart in Lucerne. The hotel was delightful, and everyone was out to see them when they left. Florie, experienced in obsequious European ways, probably had money ready to pay off the lineup. Mrs. Coolidge made no mention of that small detail. Grace liked everything about Lucerne, not least the neatness and cleanliness, reminiscent of Burlington. She admired the flower boxes in every window, the irresistible shops, including a children's store with all kinds of things for Cynthia. She saw the Lion of Lucerne, impressive.

June 14 she wrote John of a silly, funny rumor. It said she had joined the Roman Catholic church on Easter Sunday in Rome. The owner of R. H. Stearns and Son had joined the church, passing over from the Episcopalians, and this may have been the source of the rumor, which declared that Stearns's son Foster and daughter-in-law were her sponsors. The story came from a friend at home, one of whose correspondents had been in Rome.[29]

On June 20 Oliver and passengers arrived in Paris, which place does not seem to have charmed them so much as its predecessor sights. They had spent the previous week visiting châteaus, an average of four a day. They saw the cathedral, the best of them, at Chartres. They did Mont-Saint-Michel, after which Paris was anticlimactic. There was another problem with Paris: upon arrival Mrs. Coolidge heard news of the nomination of Governor Alfred (Alf) Landon of Kansas as the Republican candidate for president. The GOP, she knew, was going to lose. Florie Adams, a keen Democrat, would win.

Landon was no personage to turn back the Democratic hordes of voters led by President Roosevelt, who had bought voters by the millions with Democratic largesse. In a small way, Grace wrote, he had bought her. Two years before she told John she had a letter from Postmaster General James A. Farley saying she had come under the franking privilege, for a bill passed. She wondered to John if she came under XYQ or KLM or some National Recovery Act (NRA) code. "Graft eh?" she asked.[30]

Germany was all right; they liked Baden and may have taken the baths. Whether they followed the old-fashioned German prescription there is doubtful, which was to arrange somehow to throw up, disgorge whatever they had eaten recently, then take the baths, and end with an enormous meal.

From Germany they went to the Scandinavian countries, via Denmark, and Mrs. Coolidge so liked Sweden she placed it on a par with Switzerland. In Denmark there was an enjoyable stay that started off inauspiciously. She and Florie arrived in Copenhagen and thought there would be no trouble finding rooms at the Angleterre, but to their consternation there was none. The clerk said he would telephone around and found them rooms at a nice hotel not quite finished, but their rooms were. Then they threw themselves on the mercy of the legation, for Oliver needed an oil change. Fortunately the minister, Ruth Bryan Owen (daughter of William Jennings Bryan), was off getting married and campaigning for President Roosevelt. The chargé d'affaires was North Winship, cousin of Colonel Blanton Winship, who had been one of President Coolidge's military aides. The cousin had the legation chauffeur take Oliver to the garage, and took Mrs. Coolidge and Mrs. Adams to his house, where they met his wife and had lunch, and Mrs. Winship took them around the city. Everything turned out nicely in the absence of the minister.

After Sweden it was Germany again, Hamburg and Bremerhafen, and home on the *Bremen*'s sister ship *Europa*. They arrived in mid-August. A state department man came out and escorted them through customs. Florie paid twenty-seven dollars, Grace nothing, after which it was back in Northampton. They had been gone six months and driven 12,000 miles.

In the remaining years of the 1930s, down to that day of change in December 1941, life with Florie Adams was an incessant round of

Road Forks, Northampton, designed by Grace Coolidge and built
after the president's death in 1933.
Courtesy of the Forbes Library, Northampton, Massachusetts.

memorable times that pleased Grace Coolidge in every way. She once referred to Florie as a perfect peach, perhaps a description of pre–World War I times.[31] That may not have been true, but she assuredly admired having such a friend who enjoyed life.

The trips to the mountain continued, and Florie undertook to build a new house at the top that required months of construction. She and a relative inherited the mountaintop, and they divided it. A house already was there, the Slick Rock house, the relative desired it, and Florie took a tract at the other end of the top. It had two small buildings, and for a time she considered remodeling them but finally decided to tear them down and build under a single roof. The two women took train trips down to get the work started and drove down for the finishing of the inside. To build up there was an undertaking, for all the material had to be hauled five miles up the mountain road. The state took over the road but moved slowly in doing work on it, pounding in rock at the worst places and blasting out rock in another to eliminate a bad bridge over a ravine. At the top there was to be a caretaker's house and a two-car garage in addition to the main house. From the house, once completed, Grace

Coolidge could spend hours upon hours looking over North and South Carolina, seeing the clouds float across blue sky, or the gathering of storm clouds. It was Burlington all over again, comforting to a person who had grown up with distances and now lived once more with them. In the clouds—it is not too much to write—she could see the faces of her Calvin and of Calvin II.

The architect of the mountain house did so well that Mrs. Coolidge engaged him two years later, in 1938, to construct a house for herself in Northampton. The cost was $25,000. She described it as Road Forks because it was on a triangular lot with beautiful trees that came to a point between two streets neither of which the house faced. It was across the street from Florie. The house had unusual features. She described them with pride, for this was the first house she herself had contracted for and built to her own taste. It had no cellar. The ground floor was the utility floor, a part of it being garage, with space for three cars, hers, one from Florie's fleet, the other for a guest or the car of her chauffeur, John "Johnny Jump-up" Bukosky. At the right of the front entrance on the ground floor she had a small reception room with lavatory and coat closet. On the second floor at the left, after coming up the stairs, was her salon, as the architect was pleased to call it, with a bedroom, dressing room, and bath in back. On the right as one came up was Mrs. Coolidge's combination study and dining room, with butler's pantry and kitchen back of that. The third floor contained the guest room and bath, maid's room and bath, and a large sleeping porch where she could put the overflow. For such guests there was a dressing room and bath. The house had no attic, but the roof and some walls were insulated with rock wool so the upper rooms would be comfortable. A storeroom was on the ground floor with shelves for suitcases and built-in drawers and cupboards, as well as a vault with steel door and combination lock.[32]

Thus the years passed, in splendid activity. During this time she wrote Boone of her view of herself and how she fitted into the world in which she found herself, and the letter carried an explanation of how when she was together with her husband she lived one way and then, alone, another.[33] It was not at all because, restraint gone, she took flight. That was not her nature. She told Joel she guessed they were getting old and had just about so much living left.

They might do ten years in five. In whatever way they lived it was a great experience, "and as long as we make the most of it the great life to come appears attractive." As they rose above themselves in the struggle to overcome human weaknesses, so did their spirits grow stronger, "and that is the main objective, it seems to me."

CHAPTER 7

LATER YEARS

Northampton changed during the war, for it was home to the first naval training school for women officers. Most of its facilities, including dormitories, were at Smith College. During the war 9,000 women went through its course of training. Grace Coolidge gave up Road Forks to Captain Herbert W. and Mrs. Underwood. The captain was in charge of training of the Waves (Women Accepted for Volunteer Emergency Service), and he and Mrs. Coolidge sometimes reviewed the would-be officers, who stood in military rows while the reviewers passed down the ranks. The Underwoods did a good deal of entertaining at Mrs. Coolidge's house, and so in that regard the house became a sort of annex to the facilities at Smith. Grace Coolidge liked the Underwoods and enjoyed their presence in Northampton, although she found Mrs. Underwood a curiosity because of the manner in which the captain's wife always had something on top of her head—artificial or real flowers, feathers. On one occasion Miss Snow and Mrs. Coolidge sent her two large gardenias, and she put them on her head.[1]

Mrs. Coolidge lived with Florie Adams during most of the war years—and hence had gone in with Florence Snow on the gardenias. In 1944, Florie went to New York to be near her daughter, who, married, gave birth to Florie's first grandchild in Princeton. Miss Snow moved back to Smith, and Grace took a small house until the end of the war. When the Underwoods moved out in 1945, she returned to Road Forks, and Florie lived with her for a while until she could get a new furnace for her Northampton house across the street. Florie claimed some problem with the expense of the furnace, but for her it probably was just congenial to be with Grace until the house was ready; the furnace might have been delayed because of scarcity during the war and immediately after.

The war did not appear to affect Florie Adams, as in August 1942 she and Grace went to Boston to stay overnight, the purpose of the trip being for Florie to have her hair cut.[2] But Mrs. Coolidge eagerly took part in volunteer activities. She gave much of her time to making the hundreds of Waves under command of Captain Underwood feel at home in a strange city. She was a member of the Northampton citizens' committee for departure programs of local military selectees and was present at the railroad station when the men left for the service, presenting them with gift parcels. She was in charge of Red Cross surgical dressings work one afternoon each week at the Red Cross rooms in the old high school building where volunteer women turned out hundreds of articles for emergency first aid. She acted as a civil defense watcher and took a weekly three-hour stint with Northampton watchers; as a watcher supervisor she attended regular two-hour meetings two evenings a week and was available for duty in all blackouts and test mobilizations. No enemy planes of course appeared, but for months after the beginning of the war there was fear of raids of some sort. Pearl Harbor created a sense of danger on the West Coast, with the fleet at Hawaii crippled, and in the summer of 1942 long-range German submarines sank ships up and down the East Coast, ships silhouetted against the lights of coastal cities. Northampton was inland, but there was no telling what submarines might do, perhaps launching planes for coastal raids.

As the war wound down in 1945 with victory in Europe and approaching victory against Japan, the atomic bombs startled the country, mostly with a sense that the Japanese war could not continue. Mrs. Coolidge wrote Helen Boone that the bombs might bring an end, which they did.[3]

Peacetime allowed Northampton to go back to its ways, and for Mrs. Coolidge it became again the city she had known since she graduated from the University of Vermont in 1902 and moved to the

Grace Coolidge, post–World War II.
Courtesy of the Forbes Library,
Northampton, Massachusetts.

Clarke School, to meet her future husband. She could walk down-town from Road Forks, as from nearby Massasoit Street, but after the war preferred to use her car driven by John Bukosky. This was the Lincoln car she and the former president had bought years ear-lier, and sometimes, indeed increasingly, the sight of it brought at-tention, for it was beginning to be an antique. Mrs. Coolidge brought little attention in the city, for she was such a familiar part of it. On Main Street she visited the shops and stores as in earlier times. As Main Street came in from the east, one could turn north on King Street and stop in at the Calvin, a movie house, which Grace at-tended now and then; she once went to see Greta Garbo. Across King was the Hotel Northampton that the Waves had taken over during the war and was now back in business for visitors and espe-cially for Smith College alumnae visiting their daughters. Going west, on another side street, stood the lackluster building where on the second floor the office of Coolidge and Hemenway once had been, the door with its announcement of the firm still there. On Main Street was the turreted city hall, looking like a turn-of-the-century armory, where Mayor Coolidge once presided. On down

Main was the Academy of Music, the place for artists, musical and stage, the place where young Grace and Calvin Coolidge had attended the reception sponsored by the Daughters of the American Revolution and mistakenly sat in the chairs reserved for the then governor of Massachusetts and his lady. On the north side of Main was Edwards Church, of handsome brick construction, Gothic Victorian, inside a big tracker pipe organ, all torn down in 1957 because the congregation needed $250,000 to renovate the building and chose to construct a smaller modernistic edifice of no elegance whatsoever. To the left on Green Street stood the H. H. Richardson-designed Forbes Library of the 1890s, which in the mid-1950s would house an upstairs Coolidge Room with a collection of papers and artifacts dedicated to Northampton's most famous citizen.

It was always pleasant for the former first lady to go up or down Main Street, which she referred to as going "down street," for it was such from Road Forks and Massasoit. After the war Mrs. Coolidge remarked the decline of the city's restaurants. The Tavern, with a few timbers of an old restaurant of that purpose, now a subterranean portion of the Hotel Northampton, remained a favorite place. The problem with eating anywhere was being found by autograph hunters. In 1955, no longer getting around easily, with only two years to live, she was at the Tavern when, as she told the robins, a hunter found her:

I was having lunch there a few days ago when from the corner of my eye I saw a woman approaching. In one hand she had her paper place mat, in the other a pen. "Ah yes," I said to myself, "it's one of those." She opened up with the usual question, "Aren't you Mrs. Coolidge?" Sometimes I like to play with her ilk a little (can it be possible that I do not mind making them a little uncomfortable?). "Are you a good guesser?" I asked. She thought she was and then the same old line about recognizing me from my picture, always admired etc. and would I autograph her place mat— all this in the middle of my lunch, of course. She laid down her mat and passed me her pen. By this time my better self had taken control and I moved my plate to one side to make room for her mat and wrote my name and the date.

*Dedication of the Coolidge Room at Forbes Library, in the chapel of Smith
College, Northampton. Grace, son John, granddaughters Cynthia and Lydia,
and her daughter-in-law Florence. September 16, 1956. This would prove to be
her last formal occasion, her death coming the following year.
Courtesy of the Forbes Library, Northampton, Massachusetts.*

She made the error of asking the woman what sort of pen she offered, and the woman insisted that Mrs. Coolidge keep it. The pen was a Paper Mate and did not work—it skipped. It had a cartridge filled with sickly green ink.[4]

So some of the time went. She worked for the Edwards Church, selling aprons at bazaars. She chaired the organ fund. She worked for the Smith College fund, probably at the request of Florence Snow, also because she attended so many functions there, pouring tea. Before she and Florie went to Europe, they attended an annual series of alumnae courses, each with a theme that for 1935 was, appropriately, "Europe since 1870." Smith often honored her, as when the college carilloneur called one birthday evening to say he was going to play in honor of her birthday and that of his daughter. He played "Happy Birthday," and the wind was right and carried the sound to Road Forks, and followed with "Those Endearing Young Charms." Mrs. Coolidge waited so he could get home and called to thank him. She had calls from friends.[5]

She enjoyed visits from John and Florence and Cynthia and Lydia (born in 1938), who had moved to Farmington, a suburb of Hartford. In earlier years she went down to stay with them, but when it became difficult—"Johnny Jump-up" had to take time off from his factory job and drive her—they came to see her, sometimes on visits that extended to Plymouth Notch, where they maintained the house and farm.

She enjoyed the nearby presence of Florie, always doing something. Janey, now divorced, was back in the household. When the head of the United Mine Workers, John L. Lewis, sent his miners back to work in 1946 because of an ultimatum from President Truman, Mrs. Coolidge telephoned Florie and got Janey, who said it called for a celebration. So she "grabbed" a jar of caviar and made canapés and went over. The daughter made old-fashioneds. She stayed for supper. Later that year, close to Christmas, she went over to help with a dinner for nineteen, went over next morning for breakfast and opening of stockings. It was a family affair. One time she went over for Sunday night dinner and to see a record player and radio that had FM. That evening after dinner there was Parcheesi.[6]

At the end of the war, when Mrs. Coolidge returned to Road Forks, she learned that Ivah Gale, who had employment in White River Junction, had received "notice" and no longer could stay there. She asked Ivah to come and live with her, as Ivah had done in the year 1900, occupying the maid's room where there was a private bath. She came in September 1946. For years Mrs. Coolidge had considered Ivah as her "sister." Ivah was company and entirely unobtrusive. She now was deaf. At the outset of her long stay she wore a pince-nez. Often she was gone to Branford in Connecticut, where she stayed with her brother and his invalid wife. During one of those visits she wrote Grace of someone in or near Branford who had a systolic blood pressure of 224, which Grace thought a bit high. Mrs. Coolidge may have erred when she said she always thought the measure of blood pressure was 100 plus one's age.[7]

Vicariously she continued, as for so many years, to live with the robins. Over the last dozen years of her life the robin letters showed well her interests and concerns and, as she admitted near the end, some slowing down. In 1948 she wrote a member of the group who had gone to a nursing home that she hoped the bird would continue to find her and that the group was rooting for her. In a letter of 1952 she told a story about a little girl, one of twins four years of age, who was on the train with their father and mother. A sailor came in and took the seat back of them and was smoking (what a bygone day that was!). The little girl stood on the seat and looked him over and presently said, "Can you blow rings?" He proceeded to qualify, and with a look of approval she told him, "My daddy can do that. I don't smoke myself." In 1954 she told her friends how she enjoyed her screened-in porch with the sun shining through the autumn-colored leaves. She was in a mellow mood that she desired, she said, to pass on to all the group. "May you have a happy winter in good health with some deeds of kindness done by and for you." Her porch at Road Forks must have recalled the porch at The Beeches, which was one of the recommendations of that otherwise gloomy place.

She kept up with the news, national and international, and in 1955 related to the robins her sadness for Princess Margaret of England but could not make up her own mind if Margaret would marry the air ace in the Battle of Britain, the handsome commoner Peter Townsend. "It is going to be touch and go with her either way. I'll bet the Duchess of Windsor is going about with her fingers crossed hoping that she will, just to spite the Royal Family."

The *Springfield Union* published crossword puzzles, with prizes, and the current prize, she told the robins in 1955, was $50. If there was more than one person correctly solving the puzzle, the prize was divided. If no one solved the puzzle, the money carried over to the next week, added to that of the week before. The prize got up to $650, and a Springfield girl won it who said she needed it for her education. Grace and Ivah sent in answers and had great fun when the paper came Saturday mornings with the correct solutions. To the robins she wrote, "Just so that you may see what I am writing about I am sending along a facsimile and the clues."[8]

Television came in during the early 1950s, and she had none and did not want one. A friend told her he had one he was going to have set up for her the next week because he felt sure she did not know what she was talking about when she said she did not want one. Her objection was that so many of the interesting programs came late at night when she should be "in my downy bed."[9]

She enjoyed baseball games on the radio, and during the season she and Florie sat by the radio day after day. One time she heard herself honored as the first lady of baseball in a three-game series between the Sox and the Washington Senators, this in Boston. In a five-minute ceremony in the first game she was presented in absentia with a scroll signed by the owners and managers of both teams. The president and principal of Clarke School accepted the scroll, 100 Clarke students were in attendance, and a Clarke pitcher and catcher threw out the ball in the first game. Time was when she had gone to Fenway where her presence was duly noted, and when she was absent for too long the owner of the team sent her flowers. She and Florie and their friend Joseph D. Collins, a retired physician, would drive to Boston on Route 2, this before the Turnpike, and if necessary stay overnight. One time Florie was hit on the head by a foul ball, no harm done. The radio was no substitute for being there, but better than television, for they imagined Fenway and the crowd.[10]

For entertainment, instruction, and sometimes annoyance she read books, on which she was an unusually intelligent critic. Her husband had liked books, and when they married he brought along his small bookcase that included a memorial volume of letters and lectures of the Amherst College teacher, the mystical (he wore two overcoats in an overheated classroom because cold air was bad for his health) Charles Garman, whose lectures taught the idea of service in politics, Calvin Coolidge's reason for holding office. There is no evidence Mrs. Coolidge read Garman, whose convoluted logic would not have been a page-turner, even though her husband kept the book on a stand next to his bed in the White House. But in the 1930s when with Florie on the mountain, and while their helper Dewey was bringing in logs more than four feet long for the crackling fire—and when the two of them were not walking or playing rummy—she read serious books. She wrote John on December 31, 1934, that she was reading H. G. Wells's *Adventures in Autobiography* and found it absorbing. She had finished *Mutiny on the Bounty* and *Men against the Sea*. She and Florie were reading to each other. She told the robins in 1937, when *Gone with the Wind* was newly out, that she considered it a chore "and I became so disgusted with Scarlet that I could hardly keep my hands off her." She read Henry F. Pringle's *Life and Times of William Howard Taft,* not as enticing as his earlier book on Theodore Roosevelt; she did not say it but Taft, whom she knew when he was chief justice of the Supreme Court, was no "TR." She found extremely interesting the account of the Taft-Roosevelt break, probably for its analysis of what ambition could do to friendship. After the war she kept up, as all Washingtonians did, with the writings of Frances Parkinson Keyes, because she was the wife of the senator from New Hampshire, but became bored with Mrs. Keyes's long-drawn-out books. She wasted lots of time reading some of F. Scott Fitzgerald's crazy books and books about him, "but I keep on hoping that before I reach the end I will find out why it should be at the head of the best-seller list." In a letter to the robins she reported that when in Vermont at the Notch she read four books but could not recommend any of them. She read the *Saturday Review of Literature* and did not like it, saying, "I get very much misled by the reviews." She tried to support local writers, such as Mary Ellen Chase of Smith; when Grace and Florie went to Europe, they had seen Miss Chase, but her explanation to the robins in a letter of January 12, 1951, was unflattering: "I read part of Mary Ellen Chase's *Abby Aldrich Rockefeller* in manuscript but have not read the book. What I did read seemed to me a little thin and I think it should have been written for distribution among Mrs. Rockefeller's friends and privately printed."[11]

For Christmas 1948, Ivah was absent from Road Forks but sent Grace a book about African violets, and Mrs. Coolidge discovered the violets, which fascinated her. She found there was an African Violet Society of America, Inc., with exhibitions and bulletins to members and chapters in twenty states. In 1953 she told the robins, "I wish that you might all see my African violets which are masses of flowers." They had been in bloom for over a year, and she received four new ones for Easter, two purple, one white, one pink. "Does anyone join me in the hobby of raising African violets?"[12]

Age at last touched the former first lady, whose stunning portrait of 1924 by Howard Chandler Christy, wearing the red dress that her husband disliked, holding the white collie, Rob Roy, with the White House behind her, was now far into the past. In 1952 the first signs had appeared, in that she refused to walk distances, so unlike her. She fell asleep on a couch, unlike her. She gave up her annual visits to the Notch. In March 1955, she was taken to the hospital for two days and, as she put it, "chucked into an oxygen tent," a sign in those early days of cardiology that she suffered from heart trouble. On her next hospital visit she stayed two months. She summed up her problem: "The old pump was not working properly and my pace had to be slowed down and now I have to adjust myself to leading a more restrictive life." Ivah was there to help, and Grace got in a country girl to cook and do general housework. She lived in the lap of luxury, she said, because while she was in the hospital workmen installed "the cutest little cage" of an elevator that ran from the first to the third floor to save her walking up and down.[13]

July 7, 1957, John and Florence and the girls stopped in on the way back from Vermont en route to Connecticut. They had just gotten home when word came to return, but John's mother died twenty minutes before he arrived. It was within two hours of the anniversary of the death of Calvin Jr. in 1924. She was seventy-eight. The diagnosis was heart disease and congestive heart failure, hastened by curvature of the spine. One of her last photographs, taken September 1956, at the Smith College chapel, at the dedication of the Calvin Coolidge Memorial Room at Forbes Library, showed her standing in the aisle with John and family, quite stooped, held by the arm of her devoted son.

Everything went back to Burlington, where Grace Goodhue made her welcome appearance in 1879 and lived until graduation from the university. And the first of her principles—there were the three—was the need for order and beauty, which the town along Lake Champlain provided. Beginning with the piers and warehouses on the lake, the streets were in discernible order and rose in tiered fashion, College Street being the street of large houses and spacious yards. Maple Street, along which were the second and third Goodhue houses, was a connecting street from the lake. The town rose, properly, to the university at the top of the hill. Thence the scenery filled in both sides of Champlain—behind the university the Green Mountains, at the lower end of which, not even in the village of Plymouth Junction but in the Notch a mile into the mountains, her suitor and husband grew up. West of the lake lay the Adirondacks.

Growing up amid such scenery there was the move to Northampton, where Grace Goodhue met her Calvin. Northampton was almost flat and became home by virtue of long residence, but when it was possible to flee to scenery on the mountain near Tryon, Mrs. Coolidge did not hesitate, gazing out the huge picture window, looking to south and north, mountains again on each side, clouds scudding and casting shadows. Because of memory of the Notch, which was poetry to her husband, she appreciated the lesser slopes that came into the cluster of houses and the general store and church and cheese factory, and in her last stay there with her husband, in 1932, waxed poetic about the place in the absence of tourists and in the frost of an autumn morning.

Family was her second need, which explained much about her life. Her mother was devoted to the child, her father wonderfully permissive to a young woman who needed no discipline, and she and Ivah in winter went flying down the hill on her childhood sled, to the smile of her father, the captain of the port. When the boys were growing up in Northampton the principal awkwardness was the weekends when her political husband came home tired and snappish, his return Monday entirely welcome. Otherwise it was a household of enjoyment watching the boys grow. Hence the unspeakable sadness when Calvin II left so suddenly, his life ahead of him. Her husband told a visiting friend that heaven would be a strange place if only populated by old people, one of those intimate remarks of which he was capable, but his wife took cold comfort from that.

Devotion to family explained the heartsickness during presidential vacations at Swampscott and in the Adirondacks. She could hardly bear her husband's inability to deal with John, in every way a model son, as the years showed.

Need for family, once John married and moved to Connecticut, explained in considerable part Mrs. Coolidge's taking up with Mrs. Adams. She and Janey and Florence Snow constituted a family in Northampton. After the war it was Florie and Ivah, Grace's sister with the hearing aid and for a while the pince-nez. Crosswords, baseball, books, violets, and letters took up the time.

Lastly religion—such a foundation for life as few individuals knew even in her era when churchgoing was popular. To Joel Boone she could voice her feelings about how life was a preparation for life everlasting. She sold aprons at the Edwards Church and was chair of the music committee, seeking funds to rebuild the organ, for the music of a great organ lifted her up. People who observed her self-lessness, her humor, never the sign of appreciating the adulation that came to presidents and first ladies, said her life showed a nobil-ity. She would have sniffed at such a description, for to her—and it was a reason for her popularity—it showed only a preparation for what was to come.

NOTES

CHAPTER 1. EARLY YEARS

1. Elin L. Anderson, *We Americans: A Study of Cleavage in an American City* (Cambridge, Mass.: Harvard University Press, 1937), 10.

2. Peter Carlough, *Bygone Burlington* (Burlington, Vt.: Queen City, 1976).

3. Lawrence E. Wikander and Robert H. Ferrell, eds., *Grace Coolidge: An Autobiography* (Worland, Wyo.: High Plains, 1992), 9.

4. The Coolidges' older son, John, related his father's opinion of Mrs. Goodhue to the assistant White House physician, Joel T. Boone. Boone memoirs, XXI, 614, Boone papers, Library of Congress.

5. Description of these houses was unavailable until the early chapters of Grace Coolidge's autobiography appeared in 1992. The manuscript, in Grace Coolidge's typescript, is in the Coolidge Room of Forbes Library, the public library of Northampton.

6. *Grace Coolidge: An Autobiography,* 20.

7. Ibid., 9–10.

8. Grace Coolidge, undated (1954?), robin letters, Calvin Coolidge Memorial Foundation, Plymouth Notch, Vt. For the "robins" see below.

9. Susan Webb, "Grace Goodhue Coolidge," *The Real Calvin Coolidge* 10 (1994): 15. The author knew Cornelia Underwood.

10. The account of nine handwritten pages was for a Mr. McKenzie, apparently at the time Grace Coolidge was in the White House. Gale papers, Calvin Coolidge Memorial Foundation.

11. *American* magazine 108 (Sept., Oct., Nov., Dec. 1929): 11ff., 16ff., 20ff., 24ff.; 109 (Jan. 1930): 18ff.

12. "The Real Calvin Coolidge: A First-Hand Story of His Life, Told by 50 People Who Knew Him Best and Edited with Commentary by Grace Coolidge," *Good Housekeeping* 100 (Feb., Mar., Apr., May, June 1935): 18ff., 22ff., 28ff., 38ff., 42ff.

13. Robert V. Daniels, ed., *The University of Vermont: The First Two Hundred Years* (Hanover, N.H.: University Press of New England, 1991), chapters by T. D. Seymour Bassett, Constance M. McGovern, Virginia Campbell Downs, and Jane P. Ambrose.

14. *Burlington, Vt. and Lake Champlain: Photogravures* (Burlington, Vt.: Shanley, 1900). A copy is in the Clements Library, University of Michigan, Ann Arbor.

15. Ishbel Ross, *Grace Coolidge and Her Era: The Story of a President's Wife* (New York: Dodd, Mead, 1962), 7. "In my class in college there was a girl known as the class grind. Her name was Donna Marie Sester. She had no time nor thought for anything other than her books and her classes, nor to enter into any sort of intercourse with other students. The unusual has always interested me, particularly the unusual in people, and I somehow managed to edge myself into her consciousness and became the one friend she had in college. I didn't try to change her in any way. I didn't try to include her in the activities in which the rest of us were inclined to spend some of our time, to waste it, in her estimation, I am sure, although we never discussed it. She was the only child of parents to whom she had been born late in their lives. She didn't have an unusual mind but she had a wonderful memory. She never learned to reason as deeply as the students who had less textbook knowledge but she pulled down As from the beginning to the end of her four years. It was a strange association. I was as frivolous as she was studious and I took my parties as seriously as she did her books. She never looked disapprovingly when I went to class, sadly unprepared because I had been out dancing the night before when she had been grimly drinking at the font of knowledge. We took second-year Spanish together, the only ones in the class, and read *Don Quixote*. She sometimes came to supper at our house and we would indulge in a few bookish antics. I am sure that I was the only one in college who ever went to her house and I doubt if any of the others ever met her father and mother. Naturally she taught school after we were graduated. She lived in the household of the village pharmacist. I believe the man also sold insurance and he, undoubtedly, had other activities. I never saw him. His wife died, in the course of time, and Donna and he were married. He was much older than she. She tried to make a housewife of herself but I judge the venture wasn't altogether satisfactory so he added the housekeeping to his other duties and she went back to teaching. I used to see her when I was in Boston but I have not heard from her in years. I think her husband must have had some means and took some pride in her for she began to wear very much more modern clothes of better material and she loosened up on her really lovely hair which she had screwed back into a tight little plug, neat but taut. I am sure I should have heard from her as the years went by, if she was able to write, so I think something must have happened." Grace Coolidge to Grace Medinus, undated (Saturday before Easter, 1931), Medinus papers, Forbes Library.

16. Gale account for Mr. McKenzie, 1.

17. Ibid., 3–5.

18. Ross, *Grace Coolidge and Her Era*, 7.

19. *Grace Coolidge: An Autobiography*, 27–28.

20. Ibid., 27.

21. The robin letters from 1915 to 1920 have been lost. By the latter year Mrs. Coolidge had become prominent as the wife of the Republican candidate for the vice presidency, and one of the national officers, a robin, Anna Nickerson, saved copies from that time onward.

22. Grace Coolidge to Ivah Gale, Sept. 28, 1932, Gale papers.

23. Caroline A. Yale, *Years of Building: Memories of a Pioneer in a Special Field of Education* (New York: Dial, 1931).

24. Charlene McPhail Anderson, "Grace Coolidge and the Clarke School for the Deaf," *The Real Calvin Coolidge* 10 (1994): 5.

25. Robert V. Bruce, *Bell: Alexander Graham Bell and the Conquest of Solitude* (Boston: Little, Brown, 1973). Bell considered himself primarily a teacher of the deaf; the telephone was an incident in his larger purpose. His father-in-law, Hubbard, financed the invention.

26. *Grace Coolidge: An Autobiography*, 38.

27. Anderson, "Grace Coolidge and the Clarke School for the Deaf," 13.

28. Grace Coolidge in *Good Housekeeping* 100 (June 1935): 205.

29. *Good Housekeeping* 100 (Feb. 1935): 19.

30. Ross, *Grace Coolidge and Her Era*, 12–13.

31. Letter of Oct. 1, 1905, Gale papers.

32. *Good Housekeeping* 100 (Mar. 1935): 22.

33. Grace Coolidge in *Good Housekeeping* 100 (Mar. 1935): 22; *Grace Coolidge: An Autobiography*, 33.

34. Robert A. Woods, *The Preparation of Calvin Coolidge* (Boston: Houghton Mifflin, 1924), 46–47.

CHAPTER 2: DOUBLE HARNESS

1. For Coolidge houses, see Susan Well, "Calvin Coolidge's Homes in Northampton," Forbes Library.

2. Comment in *Good Housekeeping* 100 (Mar. 1935): 23.

3. *Grace Coolidge: An Autobiography*, 36.

4. Frank L. Stoddard, *As I Knew Them: Presidents and Politics from Grant to Coolidge* (New York: Harper, 1927), 531–532.

5. Boone memoirs, XXI, 951–952.

6. Woods, *The Preparation of Calvin Coolidge*, 132.

7. See "Mrs. Coolidge Writes Cook Book Recipes for Congressional Club's Favorite Dishes," *New York Times*, Sept. 16, 1927. She gave recipes for custard pie and corn muffins.

8. *Grace Coolidge: An Autobiography*, 56–58; *Good Housekeeping* 100 (May 1935): 250.

9. Ross, *Grace Coolidge and Her Era*, 25.

10. *Grace Coolidge: An Autobiography*, 33, 35.

11. Boone memoirs, XXI, 49–51, 54, 184, 326, 608.

12. Introduction to Edward Connery Lathem, ed., *Your Son, Calvin Coolidge: A Selection of Letters from Calvin Coolidge to His Father* (Montpelier: Vermont Historical Society, 1968), v.

13. Ross, *Grace Coolidge and Her Era*, 36.

14. *Grace Coolidge: An Autobiography*, 45–46.

15. Boone memoirs, XXII, 74.

16. *Grace Coolidge: An Autobiography*, 94; *Good Housekeeping* 100 (Mar. 1935): 219.

17. *Good Housekeeping* 100 (Mar. 1935): 219.

18. For its subject, see Francis Russell, *A City in Terror: 1919, the Boston Police Strike* (New York: Viking, 1975). It overdraws the danger of disorder and is hostile to Coolidge. An evenhanded account is in Donald R. McCoy, *Calvin Coolidge: The Quiet President* (New York: Macmillan, 1967). Coolidge's feeling after his statement to Gompers, that he had hurt himself politically, has a thin documentation. He appears to have told this to the governor of Vermont, Percival W. Clement, similarly to his stepmother at Plymouth Notch. The informing of the Vermont governor was remarked by a cabinet member in the 1930s; the letter to the stepmother has not survived.

19. Horace Green, *The Life of Calvin Coolidge* (New York: Duffield, 1924), 67.

20. Claude M. Fuess, *Calvin Coolidge: The Man from Vermont* (Boston: Little, Brown, 1940), 264–265.

21. To Therese Hills, undated (1920), Hills papers.

22. Undated letters (1921), Hills papers.

23. Ibid.

24. *Grace Coolidge: An Autobiography*, 59–60.

25. Ibid., 55.

26. Letter of Apr. 15, 1921, Hills papers.

27. Frances Parkinson Keyes, *Capital Kaleidoscope: The Story of a Washington Hostess* (New York: Harper, 1937), 122.

28. Undated letter (1921), Hills papers.

29. Theodore Roosevelt Jr. diary, Aug. 3, 1923, Roosevelt papers, Library of Congress; box 21, papers of Dean Albertson, University of Massachusetts archives, Amherst, Massachusetts.

30. Undated letter (1921), Hills papers.

31. Curtis said this to a reporter, with an injunction that it was not to be published until after his death. *New York Times,* Feb. 9, 1936. Dawes refused comment.

32. Nicholas Murray Butler, *Across the Busy Years: Recollections and Reflections,* 2 vols. (New York: Scribner's, 1939–1940), 1:355–356.

33. Fuess, *Calvin Coolidge,* 293.

34. Keyes, *Capital Kaleidoscope,* 88.

35. Woods, *The Preparation of Calvin Coolidge,* 215; Green, *The Life of Calvin Coolidge,* 177–178.

CHAPTER 3: "SHE TOOK PRECEDENCE OVER ME"

1. *Grace Coolidge, An Autobiography,* 62.

2. By Cosmopolitan, then a New York publisher as sponsor of the well-known magazine.

3. The best source for both first ladies is Stacy E. Cordery's sketches in Lewis L. Gould, ed., *First Ladies: Their Lives and Their Legacy* (New York: Garland, 1996).

4. The best source for Edith Wilson is the editor's own sketch in his *First Ladies* (quotation, 363). The literature on the second Mrs. Wilson, in articles and books, is large.

5. Edith Wilson, *My Memoir* (Indianapolis: Bobbs Merrill, 1939).

6. Robert H. Ferrell, *The Strange Deaths of President Harding* (Columbia: University of Missouri Press, 1996); the present writer does not agree with the innuendo of Carl Sferrazza Anthony, *Florence Harding: The First Lady, the Jazz Age, and the Death of America's Most Scandalous President* (New York: Morrow, 1998).

7. Mary Randolph, *Presidents and First Ladies* (New York: Appleton-Century, 1935), is filled with her experiences.

8. Letter of Mar. 25, 1927.

9. Boone memoirs, XXI, 741–742; "The Real Calvin Coolidge," *Good Housekeeping* 100 (June 1935); query in article by Derieux and comment by Grace Coolidge.

10. According to the *New York Times,* Apr. 26, 1925, Mrs. Coolidge searched the White House storehouse and resurrected two items that had been discarded. One was a table inset with brass diagonal pieces, save for a missing piece. She

had it restored. She picked up an old-fashioned comfortable chair bearing a tag, "President Jackson's chair," which she placed in her husband's second-floor study. For her second attempt, through Mrs. Lorimer, *Washington Post,* Mar. 28, 1926, and its squelching by the White House spokesman, Mar. 31. In 1931 she wrote her friend Grace Medinus three times (two letters undated, the third of September 26) about her frustration. In the third she described photographs sent her from a woman in Springfield, Vermont, of a Duncan Phyfe sewing table in perfect condition that the woman wished to sell for $10,000. The woman wanted to sell because she had no resources. Later one sold in New York for twice that. If Mrs. Coolidge had the money, she said, she would buy it, for it was just the sort of thing for the White House. (Given prices for first-rate antiques, perhaps part of the reason the proposal for donated antiques to the White House failed was reluctance of owners to give them up in view of their value.)

11. For the roof and changes, see William Seale, *The President's House: A History,* 2 vols. (Washington, D.C., and New York: White House Historical Association, National Geographic Society, and Harry N. Abrams, 1986), 2:852–884; Seale, *The White House: The History of an Idea* (Washington, D.C.: American Institute of Architects and White House Historical Association, 1992), 211–217.

12. *Grace Coolidge: An Autobiography,* 80–81.

13. Robert H. Ferrell, ed., *Off the Record: The Private Papers of Harry S. Truman* (New York: Harper and Row, 1980), 242–245.

14. Boone memoirs, XXI, 29, 307, 369–370.

15. Grace Coolidge in *Good Housekeeping* 100 (Mar. 1935), 217.

16. Ibid., 217–218.

17. Ross, *Grace Coolidge and Her Era,* 147.

18. *New York Times,* Sept. 25, 1927.

19. Randolph, *Presidents and First Ladies,* 74–75.

20. *Washington Post,* Dec. 16, 1923.

21. *New York Times,* Sept. 25, 1927.

22. *New York Times,* Nov. 6, 1927.

23. Boone memoirs, XXI, 183–184; Keyes, *Capital Kaleidoscope,* 127–128.

24. *New York Times,* May 4, 1924.

25. Oct. 27, 1928.

26. Keyes, *Capital Kaleidoscope,* 124, 211.

27. Robin letters, 1927.

28. *New York Times,* Apr. 20, 1927.

29. *New York Times,* May 7, 1927; Vera Bloom, *There's No Place Like Washington* (New York: Putnam's, 1944), 20, 25, 32.

30. *Washington Post,* Feb. 26, 1929.

31. *New York Times,* Feb. 27, 1929.

CHAPTER 4: PUBLIC EVENTS

1. Grace Coolidge, Nov. 26, 1923, robin letters.

2. Fuess, *Calvin Coolidge,* 367.

3. Grace Coolidge, Nov. 26, 1923, robin letters.

4. Robert H. Ferrell, "The Expanding White House: Creating the East and West Wings," in *The White House: The First Two Hundred Years,* ed. Frank Freidel and William Pencak (Boston: Northeastern University Press, 1994), 100–111.

5. Eugene F. Trani, *The Treaty of Portsmouth: An Adventure in American Diplomacy* (Lexington: University Press of Kentucky, 1969), 120–123.

6. *Grace Coolidge: An Autobiography,* 88–90. The first lady wrote of the church services, "A special blessing seemed to rest upon the little company assembled to worship God, and something of the religious zeal which brought our Pilgrim forefathers across the mighty ocean came to me during those services on board the good ship which bore the name of theirs."

7. To Grace Medinus, undated (1931), Medinus papers, Forbes Library.

8. Elise K. Kirk, *Music at the White House: A History of the American Spirit* (Urbana: University of Illinois Press, 1986), 198–220.

9. "Dr. Rachmaninoff came and played for me a week ago today. I had about three hundred in for the music and the tea." Undated letter, robin letters.

10. Randolph, *Presidents and First Ladies,* 140.

11. Box 19, "Programs of receptions and dinners at the White House," Forbes Library.

12. Boone memoirs, XXI, 734ff.

13. Edmund W. Starling, *Starling of the White House: The Story of the Man Whose Secret Service Detail Guarded Five Presidents from Woodrow Wilson to Franklin D. Roosevelt* (New York: Simon and Schuster, 1946), 219.

14. *New York Times,* May 8, 1927.

15. *Washington Post,* Nov. 26, 1923.

16. *Washington Post,* Dec. 17, 1924.

17. *New York Times,* June 20, 1926.

18. Announced in *New York Times,* Jan. 26, 1929.

19. Ross, *Grace Coolidge and Her Era,* 152–154.

20. *New York Times,* Mar. 18, 1921.

21. *Washington Post,* Apr. 24, 1925.

22. *Washington Post,* Mar 11, 1926.

23. *Washington Post,* Mar. 11, 1926.

24. *Washington Post,* Nov. 21, 1926.

25. Gloria May Stoddard, *Grace and Cal: A Vermont Love Story* (Shelburne, Vt.: New England Press, 1989), 109.

26. *New York Times,* Mar. 25, 1925.

27. Stoddard, *Grace and Cal,* 107–109.

28. *New York Times,* Nov. 12, 1948.

29. *Daily Hampshire Gazette,* July 8, 1957.

30. *New York Times,* Nov. 1, 1923.

31. *Washington Herald-Times,* June 9, 1926, Hannay collection.

32. *New York Times,* Sept. 5, 1923.

33. *New York Times,* June 6, 1925.

34. *New York Times,* Aug. 26, 1926.

35. *New York Times,* June 6, 1927.

36. *New York Times,* Feb. 2, 1929.

37. *New York Times,* Aug. 23, 1927.

38. *New York Times,* Dec. 23, 1926.

CHAPTER 5: THE FAMILY

1. Grace Coolidge to Therese Hills, undated (Feb. 1921), Hills papers.

2. Grace Coolidge to Therese Hills, June 10, 1921, Hills papers.

3. Grace Coolidge to Therese Hills, Sept. 16, 1921, Hills papers.

4. Microfilm roll 2, Coolidge papers, Forbes Library.

5. Boone memoirs, XXI, 66.

6. Ibid., 199ff.

7. Letter on fathers to "Dear Friend," Aug. 16, 1923, microfilm roll 2, Coolidge papers, Forbes Library.

8. Undated letter (Aug. 1924), robin letters.

9. Letter of May 9, box 30, Boone papers, Library of Congress.

10. Quoted in Cynthia D. Bittinger, *Grace Coolidge: Sudden Star* (New York: Nova, 2005), 104.

11. One of the consultants brought in during the youth's illness, John A. Kolmer of Johns Hopkins, years later published an account relating that the president broke down. Visiting with Mrs. Coolidge in Northampton, Boone discussed the article, and afterward she wrote her son John about it: "At no time did your father give any outward indication of his inward suffering." Letter of Aug. 21, 1955, box 30, Boone papers.

12. July 21, 1924, microfilm roll 3, Coolidge papers, Forbes Library.

13. Lathem, *Your Son, Calvin Coolidge,* 216.

14. *The Autobiography of Calvin Coolidge* (New York: Cosmopolitan, 1929), 190.

15. Ira R. T. Smith, *"Dear Mr. President . . .": The Story of Fifty Years in the White House Mail Room* (New York: Messner, 1949), 132–133.

16. Starling, *Starling of the White House,* 224.

17. *Grace Coolidge: An Autobiography,* 93; *New York Times,* Aug. 9, 1925.

18. Boone memoirs, XXI, 463.

19. Ibid., 459.

20. Ibid., 460.

21. Ibid., 632.

22. Ibid., 567–609.

23. Starling, *Starling of the White House,* 252–253.

24. Boone memoirs, XXI, 839–852.

25. Ibid., 584–585, 850.

26. Haley so told Boone. Ibid., 847–850.

27. Homer E. Socolofsky, *Arthur Capper: Publisher, Politician, and Philanthropist* (Lawrence: University Press of Kansas, 1962), 159.

28. *Grace Coolidge: An Autobiography,* 64.

29. Boone memoirs, XXI, 930–938.

30. Ibid., 939.

31. To Therese Hills, undated (Apr. 1927), Hills papers; Boone memoirs, XXI, 944, 950–956, 975.

32. Microfilm roll 2, Coolidge papers, Forbes Library. In 1987 the present writer spoke one Sunday afternoon in the church at Plymouth Notch, and John and Florence Coolidge were present. I read from the collection of papers stored in the attic of the house at the Notch, which John Coolidge had given to Forbes Library, and quoted the correspondence between father and son concerning expenses, including the presidential letter of June 11, 1927. John Coolidge chuckled audibly. For the papers, see Lawrence E. Wikander, ed., *A Guide to the Personal Files of President Calvin Coolidge* (Northampton, Mass.: Forbes Library, 1986).

33. "The next day Mrs. Coolidge told me that John—he had ridden home to Northampton from Plainville [Connecticut] with us the night before—had commented to her that he didn't see how she put up living with his father sometimes. John had told his intimate friend Jack Hills that he (John Coolidge) was more like his father in disposition as he grew older. That worried him very much." Undated (Mar.–Apr. 1928), Boone memoirs, XXI, 975.

34. For the Coolidge Fund the best source is the microfilm of the Northampton *Daily Hampshire Gazette* in Forbes Library, notably for Nov. 16, 1928, listing

major contributors, and Mar. 13, 1929, an account of turning over the receipts of the drive to Miss Yale. New York and Washington papers carried accounts of raising the fund, but they apparently were done by stringers or copied from rivals' stories and are inaccurate.

35. Boone oral history by Raymond Henle, Herbert Hoover Library, West Branch, Iowa.

CHAPTER 6: TOGETHER, ALONE

1. Ross, *Grace Coolidge and Her Era*, 29.

2. Grace Coolidge to Therese Hills, undated (July 1931), Hills papers.

3. Grace Coolidge in "The Real Calvin Coolidge," *Good Housekeeping* 100 (Apr. 1935): 201–202.

4. Grace Coolidge to the robins, Nov. 8, 1930, robin letters.

5. Ibid.

6. W. R. Swanberg, *Citizen Hearst: A Biography of William Randolph Hearst* (New York: Scribner's, 1961), 416.

7. To Maude Trumbull, Jan. 29, 1933, Maude Trumbull papers, Coolidge Foundation.

8. To Grace Medinus, Apr. 21, 1930, box 2, Medinus papers.

9. Apr. 23, 1930, box 30, Boone papers.

10. Apr. 21, 1930, box 2, Medinus papers.

11. Sept., 28, 1932, Gale papers; Grace Coolidge to Joel T. Boone, May 27, 1932, box 30, Boone papers.

12. Sept. 27, 1932, Maude Trumbull papers.

13. To Grace Medinus, Jan. 26, Mar. 27, 1932, Medinus papers.

14. Hills papers.

15. Grace Coolidge to the robins, Oct. 4, 1929, robin letters.

16. Ibid., Nov. 8, 1930.

17. Sept. 28, 1932, Gale papers.

18. Grace Coolidge to John Coolidge, undated (Aug. 1932), John Coolidge papers.

19. Howard F. McMains, ed., "Harry New's Secret Visit to Calvin Coolidge: A 1932 Election Memoir," *Vermont History* 53 (Fall 1985): 221–230.

20. Oct. 5, 1932, box 3, Medinus papers.

21. To Edward T. Clark, "Coolidge, Calvin," box 3, Clark papers; Charles A. Andrews in "The Real Calvin Coolidge," *Good Housekeeping* 100 (June 1935): 209; Starling, *Starling of the White House*, 302.

22. Letter of Jan. 24, 1931, box 30, Boone papers.

23. Bittinger, *Grace Coolidge,* 107.

24. To John Coolidge, undated (Apr. 1934), John Coolidge papers.

25. Ibid.

26. For smoking, Irwin H. Hoover notes, microfilm roll 8, Irwin H. Hoover papers, Library of Congress.

27. Sept. 18, 1938, box 30, Boone papers.

28. To John Coolidge, Mar. 8, 15, Apr. 26, May 10, June 7, 21, Aug. 4, 16, 31, 1938, and undated, John Coolidge papers; to Joel T. Boone, Mar. 2 (postcard), box 30, Boone papers; to Ivah Gale, Apr. 28, Gale papers; to the robins, Oct. 3, robin letters.

29. John Coolidge papers.

30. Letter of June 25, 1934, John Coolidge papers.

31. Letter to Boone, Feb. 14, 1934, box 30, Boone papers.

32. Ibid., Jan. 4, 1938.

33. Letter of July 6, 1934.

CHAPTER 7: LATER YEARS

1. To Maude Trumbull, Jan. 6, 1943, Maude Trumbull papers.

2. Grace Coolidge to the robins, Aug. 12, 1942, robin letters.

3. Box 30, Boone papers.

4. To the robins, July 28, 1955, robin letters.

5. To Ivah Gale, Jan. 3, 1947, Gale papers.

6. Ibid., undated (Dec. 1946).

7. Ibid., Dec. 29, 1949.

8. To the robins, May 10, 1955, robin letters.

9. Jan. 26, 1957.

10. David Pietrusza, "Grace Coolidge: The First Lady of Baseball," *The Real Calvin Coolidge* 10 (1994): 23–26.

11. To John Coolidge, undated (Dec. 1934), John Coolidge papers; to the robins, June 29, 1937, robin letters; to John Coolidge, undated (Dec. 1939), John Coolidge papers; to the robins, undated, robin letters; to the robins, Jan. 12, 1951, robin letters.

12. To Ivah Gale, Dec., 28, 1948, Gale papers; to the robins, Apr. 13, 1953, robin letters.

13. To the robins, May 10, 1955, and undated, robin letters.

BIBLIOGRAPHIC ESSAY

The sources for a biography of Grace Coolidge are scattered, some in book form, a few in articles, much information in Mrs. Coolidge's voluminous letters—she explained in her autobiography that her letters never would be worth anything because she wrote so many. And then there was her coverage in newspapers, of any public event whether in the White House or elsewhere. It was more than that of her predecessors and, for that matter, her successors, including the peripatetic Eleanor Roosevelt. Her activities captivated Americans of the time.

BOOKS

The best place to start in published literature is Mrs. Coolidge's memoir, published for the first time in Lawrence E. Wikander and Robert H. Ferrell, eds., *Grace Coolidge: An Autobiography* (Worland, Wyo.: High Plains, 1992). Chapters for the presidency appeared in *American* magazine for January–July 1930. The editors mistakenly thought that the account of her life in Burlington and Northampton prior to that time would not interest readers, and left it out. A chapter on Coolidge pets, those of herself and her husband in the White House, is not in the Wikander and Ferrell edition, for we believed as did the *American* magazine editors that it would not engage readers—a long rundown of raccoons and dogs and cats, each with a name. The memoir is available in full at Forbes Library, the public library of Northampton, which contains a miscellany of papers, newspaper clippings, and memorabilia pertaining to both Coolidges.

Two biographies of the first lady of 1923–1929 are much worth attention. The first, Ishbel Ross, *Grace Coolidge and Her Era: The Story of a President's Wife* (New York: Dodd, Mead, 1962), rewards close reading. The author was a professional writer, an adult in the Coolidge era, and specialized in presidential wives, among other subjects a book on the second Mrs. Wilson entitled *The Power of Grace*, an interesting title for the opinionated Edith Wilson. One may only describe the Ross book on Grace Coolidge by saying that it represented careful investigation, including a visit of length to Forbes Library, where the author saw and used the then substantially unpublished Grace Coolidge memoir. She interviewed Mrs. Coolidge's surviving contemporaries. The problem with the resultant book was twofold, that Ross had a habit of stopping her narrative for long discourses on events of the time, of little or no interest in a biography of Grace Coolidge, and (see below, description of manuscript collections relating to Mrs. Coolidge) could not use manuscript collections not then available, notably one not opened until 1995, the huge memoirs of Mrs. Coolidge's White House physician, Joel T. Boone.

The second biography worth mentioning is Cynthia D. Bittinger, *Grace Coolidge: Sudden Star* (New York: Nova, 2005). The author saw the Boone papers in the Library of Congress and the many other collections unavailable to Miss Ross, including of course papers later in the Calvin Coolidge Memorial Foundation domiciled in the basement of the church in Plymouth Notch, also papers in Forbes Library. Cynthia Bittinger is executive director of the Calvin Coolidge Memorial Foundation.

The biographies of Mrs. Coolidge's husband have little about the first lady: William Allen White, *A Puritan in Babylon: The Story of Calvin Coolidge* (New York: Macmillan, 1938); Claude M. Fuess, *Calvin Coolidge: The Man from Vermont* (Boston: Little, Brown, 1940); Donald R. McCoy, *Calvin Coolidge: The Quiet President* (New York: Macmillan, 1967); Robert H. Ferrell, *The Presidency of Calvin Coolidge* (Lawrence: University Press of Kansas, 1998); David Greenberg, *Calvin Coolidge* (New York: Times/Holt, 2006). The White book is anti-Coolidge, almost venomous, often inaccurate. The Fuess is highly accurate but has little of value on the presidency, for which sources then were unavailable. For full biographies McCoy's is the best, but McCoy could not use the Boone papers, then closed. The book by the present author makes full use of Boone's memoirs and other papers but is limited to its subject. The Greenberg is a well-done survey.

The following books touch on Mrs. Coolidge, often informatively: Edmund W. Starling, *Starling of the White House: The Story of the Man Whose Secret Service Detail Guarded Five Presidents from Woodrow Wilson to Franklin D. Roosevelt* (New York: Simon and Schuster, 1946), invariably accurate, with some account of Mrs. Coolidge; Ira R. T. Smith, *"Dear Mr. President . . .": The Story of Fifty Years in the White*

House Mail Room (New York: Messner, 1949), similarly so, although it deals mostly with its subject, the presidents from McKinley to FDR; Howard H. Quint and Robert H. Ferrell, eds., *The Talkative President: The Off-the-Record Press Conferences of Calvin Coolidge* (Amherst: University of Massachusetts Press, 1964), a distillation of the verbatim press conference transcripts in Forbes Library, opened for Ferrell by the then director at Forbes, Wikander, in 1950; Robert E. Gilbert, "Psychological Pain in the White House: The Case of Calvin Coolidge," *Political Psychology* 9 (Mar. 1988): 75–100, expanded by its author into *The Mortal Presidency: Illness and Anguish in the White House* (New York: Fordham University Press, 1992), which contends that the president never recovered from the death of the Coolidges' younger son in 1924. Allison Lockwood, *A President in a Two-Family House: Calvin Coolidge of Northampton* (Northampton, Mass.: Northampton Historical Society, 1988), is a short, touching account of the Massasoit house by a former resident of Number 12 who recalls the street in the 1950s, when memory was close to the time of the Coolidges' residence. As a child she watched the president's funeral at Edwards Church, from a vantage point across from the church on Main Street.

The best book on first ladies from Martha Washington to the twentieth century is Betty Boyd Caroli, *First Ladies* (New York: Oxford University Press, 1987). For the last century it is Lewis L. Gould, ed., *First Ladies: Their Lives and Their Legacy* (New York: Garland, 1996). Built on the fact that if the name "first lady" dated to President Taylor's definition of Dolley Madison at the time of her death in 1849, the institution itself, with duties and responsibilities, although holders of the office did not always assume them, begins with President Theodore Roosevelt's wife Edith in 1902 with the refurbished White House of McKim; this excellent book by first-rate contributors, including especially the editor (Edith Wilson), covers the ground with imagination and even flair; no other first ladies book is comparable.

For the Coolidge era the book by the social secretary beginning in 1925 and before that White House assistant secretary, before that Grace Coolidge's part-time secretary during her time as wife of the vice president, Mary Randolph, *Presidents and First Ladies* (New York: Appleton-Century, 1935), is in a class by itself. A fine White House secretary, experienced in Washington society, Miss Randolph is clearly the author of record. Two other books frequently consulted by researchers are of very limited value: Elizabeth Jaffray, *Secrets of the White House* (New York: Cosmopolitan, 1927), and Irwin H. (Ike) Hoover, *Forty-two Years in the White House* (Boston: Houghton Mifflin, 1934). Both give evidence of being written in their respective publishers' offices. Mrs. Coolidge heartily disliked the Jaffray tell-all, and although she appears favorably in the Ike Hoover book, her husband does not.

For their special subjects, see William Seale, *The President's House: A History*, 2 vols. (Washington, D.C., and New York: White House Historical Association, National Geographic Society, and Harry N. Abrams, 1986); Seale, *The White House: The History of an Idea* (Washington, D.C.: American Institute of Architects and White House Historical Association, 1992); and Elise R. Kirk, *Music at the White House: A History of the American Spirit* (Urbana: University of Illinois Press, 1986). Individuals in the 1920s who knew and appraised Grace Coolidge were Frances Parkinson Keyes, *Capital Kaleidoscope: The Story of a Washington Hostess* (New York: Harper, 1937); Keyes, *All Flags Flying* (New York: McGraw-Hill, 1972); and Vera Bloom, *There's No Place Like Washington* (New York: Putnam's, 1944).

For Grace Coolidge's activities during her lifetime books of value are few. But there is much reason to consult Robert V. Bruce, *Bell: Alexander Graham Bell and the Conquest of Solitude* (Boston: Little, Brown, 1973), for the lipreading, visible speech, taught at the Clarke School; the author used to great advantage the Bell papers at the National Geographic Society in Washington. Homer E. Socolofsky, *Arthur Capper: Publisher, Politician, and Philanthropist* (Lawrence: University Press of Kansas, 1962), relates Capper's visit to the summer White House in the Black Hills in 1927. Milton F. Heller Jr., *The President's Doctor: An Insider's View of Three First Families* (New York: Vantage, 2000), uses the Boone memoirs and the White House physician's other papers to offer much information about what Boone learned from his close relationship with Mrs. Coolidge and from the president himself, to whom the doctor also administered.

ARTICLES

The article literature of value concerning Grace Coolidge is slight, for despite the plentiful publication of newspaper accounts those in periodical literature are few and for the most part of little value, being short and uninformative.

An early account, written probably by the editors of the periodical but with information obtained by the author, with assistance of her subject, is Lou Henry Hoover, "When Mrs. Coolidge Was a Girl," *American Girl* 6 (Nov. 1926); with an aversion to any account possibly raising a political issue, President Coolidge refused to allow any reprinting of this article outside of the official Girl Scout magazine. Mrs. Hoover was a longtime advocate of the Girl Scouts, and it was natural for her to solicit it. After the president's death Mrs. Coolidge brought out "The Real Calvin Coolidge: A First-Hand Story of His Life, Told by 50 People Who Knew Him Best and Edited with Commentary by Grace Coolidge," *Good Housekeeping* 100 (Feb., Mar., Apr., May, June 1935): 18ff., 22ff., 28ff., 38ff., 82ff. A few of the articles touched Mrs. Coolidge's experiences, similarly her commentaries. Susan Webb, "Grace Goodhue Coolidge," *The Real Calvin Coolidge* 10 (1994): 15–22, recalls the author's Burlington, where she met Mrs. Coolidge at age thirteen. The periodical is an occasional publication of the Calvin Coolidge Memorial Foundation at Plymouth Notch. See also Daisy Mathias and Robert Nelson, "The Beeches," *The Real Calvin Coolidge* 5 (1987), 27–29; the authors owned The Beeches. John E. Haynes, "The Calvin Coolidge Papers in the Library of Congress," *The Real Calvin Coolidge* 8 (1990), 17–26, describes the skimpiness of the papers left to the library as official papers, accompanying those of many other American presidents deposited there. Haynes is the accessions head of the Manuscript Division of the library. For its subject see Charlene McPhail Anderson, "Grace Coolidge and the Clarke School for the Deaf," *The Real Calvin Coolidge* 10 (1994): 5–13. Similarly, David Pietrusza, "Grace Coolidge: The First Lady of Baseball," *The Real Calvin Coolidge* 10 (1994): 23–26.

MANUSCRIPT COLLECTIONS

Florence Adams papers, Forbes Library. This is a disappointing collection but predictably so, for despite the closeness between Mrs. Adams and Mrs. Coolidge beginning in 1933, Grace Coolidge's friend was an activist, no writer of letters. On Mrs. Coolidge's side their proximity on Massasoit Street, and use of the telephone between households when not together, made letters virtually unnecessary. The Adams papers appear as a collection in Forbes but are few and uninteresting.

Joel T. Boone papers, Library of Congress. Opened in 1995, these papers are essential to any biographer of Mrs. Coolidge—and for that matter of her husband the president. A biographer of Florence Harding whose book appeared not long after the Boone papers became available, Carl Sferrazza Anthony, has written that he arranged for the papers to open. My understanding is that the chief archivist of the Herbert Hoover Library in West Branch, Iowa, Dwight Miller, attended to the papers' opening. The Library of Congress had been unable to get in touch with Boone's daughter Suzanne, losing her address. Miller at West Branch had an oral history of Boone and gave the Library of Congress the address of Suzanne, married to Milton F. Heller Jr.; Suzanne had died in 1991. Meanwhile, the present writer knew the contents of the Boone papers although those papers were not open; the library maintains files of its papers, and the entire calendar of the Boone papers was in its vertical files, even though out of the papers' nearly 100 boxes only two were open, of Boone's arbitration of a dispute in the Pennsylvania coalfields after World War II. In the calendar it was clear that Boone had kept a diary during the 1920s and that his memoirs comprised a thousand pages on each of the Republican presidents of the period. I asked Miller to see if there was any reason why the Boone papers in Washington could not be opened, and he duly inquired. It turned out that the memoirs consisted of taped reminiscences by the vice admiral (he was a career marine, retiring after World War II). A stenographer typed the memoirs double-spaced. Based on the line-a-day diary of the 1920s, they displayed an utterly remarkable memory, so much so that one might have thought their author made up his long accounts of Presidents Harding, Coolidge, and Hoover, except that everything available elsewhere on those presidents backed up the memoirs. Much of the dictation is dull and unimportant, but the memoirs have intimate accounts of the White House in 1923–1929. The Boone papers contain, incidentally, in box 30 (these are standard archival boxes, five inches wide), 104 Grace Coolidge letters. The papers are not on site in the Manuscript Division, and researchers must ask for boxes to be brought in from storage, which requires at least one day's notice to the library. The collection ranges widely and has many piquant observations about Boone's predecessor in the White House during the Wilson era, Rear Admiral Cary T. Grayson. Boone knew Grayson well and was not fond of him, said he often was in Grayson's office in the Naval Dispensary in Washington, where he saw the admiral's desk strewn with unopened medical journals. He believed Grayson turned against him in

1933 and made possible the appointment of Ross T. McIntire as President Roosevelt's personal physician.

John Bukosky papers, Forbes Library. Bukosky was the Coolidges' driver in Northampton after the presidency. The collection is slight, with a few notes from Mrs. Coolidge.

Calvin Coolidge papers, Forbes Library. In 1983–1984, after discovery of 104 files of Coolidge's papers in the attic of the Notch house, some of them in poor condition, having been chewed by mice, John Coolidge gave the files to Forbes. Under its former director, Wikander, who had retired as librarian of Williams College, Forbes microfilmed the papers; see Wikander's *Guide to the Personal Files of President Calvin Coolidge* (Northampton, Mass.: Forbes Library, 1986). How the papers went to the attic is unclear; they seem to have been sequestered from papers that went to the Library of Congress Manuscript Division (see below) but without any clear reason. They certainly were part of the White House Coolidge files. They are in twelve microfilm reels and available in a few large libraries around the country that purchased them from Forbes. In 1933, Edward T. Clark, Coolidge's personal secretary, said that it was Coolidge's desire to destroy everything in the so-called personal files. Five years later Mrs. Coolidge told the chief of the Manuscript Division of the Library of Congress that her husband had destroyed his personal papers. Wikander thought these files were saved by chance. The papers contain trivial things, such as invitations for honorary memberships. They also contain the president's correspondence with his son John when the latter was a student at Amherst College. Readers may find helpful Kerry W. Buckley, comp., *Guide to the Microfilm Edition of the Calvin Coolidge Papers contained in the Coolidge Collection of the Forbes Library, Northampton, Massachusetts* (Northampton: Forbes Library, 1993). The present biographer found this guide useless.

Calvin Coolidge papers, Library of Congress. The entire collection has been microfilmed, similar to most of the library's presidential collections. It has been indexed. But the papers themselves are an odd assortment of uninteresting material. Many libraries around the country have bought this presidential microfilm.

Calvin Coolidge letters to his father, John C. Coolidge, Vermont Historical Society. Here the best resort is Edward Connery Lathem, ed., *Your Son, Calvin Coolidge: A Selection of Letters from Calvin Coolidge to His Father* (Montpelier: Vermont Historical Society, 1968). Scrupulously edited, with notes from local newspapers explaining issues referred to, the letters show the devotion of father and son.

John Coolidge papers, Calvin Coolidge Memorial Foundation. Two hundred letters from the 1930s and later. Excellent for Mrs. Coolidge's trip to Europe in 1936 and informative on other subjects.

Bess Furman papers, Library of Congress. By a Washington newspaperwoman interested in first ladies, the papers are of little value as they have no working notes and only offer a rundown of the author's life.

Ivah Gale papers, Calvin Coolidge Memorial Foundation. The papers contain the Grace Coolidge letter written just before the marriage in 1905. Miss Gale later wrote nine pages of memories of college years with the then Grace Goodhue.

Therese C. Hills papers, Forbes Library. Voluminous through the vice presidency, the exchanges thin out during the presidential years when Grace Coolidge was too busy to write. After the Coolidges returned to Northampton, Mrs. Hills found herself virtually estranged from her friend, and letters almost cease after 1932.

Irwin H. Hoover papers, Library of Congress. The account after 1921 in Hoover's much-cited book seems written from the papers by editors at Houghton Mifflin. The papers for the Coolidge years are occasional, and the editors appear to have chosen whatever showed Hoover's displeasure with President Coolidge.

Grace G. Medinus papers, Forbes Library. For a short time, the late 1920s and especially in 1929–1933, in the interval between the near lapse of relations between Mrs. Coolidge and Mrs. Hills and the sudden appearance of Florence Adams, the Medinus papers show Mrs. Coolidge's life in detail. Mrs. Medinus, resident in Chicago, wrote at first about a "coverlet for the ages," which she was knitting for a bed in the Chicago Historical Society used by Abraham Lincoln; Mrs. Coolidge was attempting a similar coverlet on which she placed her name and the interesting dates of her being first lady, in which she crocheted 1923–1929. This she may well have done before her husband forsook a second full presidential term during the vacation in 1927 in the Black Hills. Grace Coolidge wrote to Mrs. Medinus at great length, and one letter is ten single-spaced pages, typescript. The collection contains nine boxes, with thirty-five Coolidge letters in box 3.

Ellen A. Riley papers, Vermont Division for Historic Preservation, Plymouth Notch. Miss Riley was dietitian after Elizabeth Jaffray, brought in from the R. H. Stearns store in Boston. The papers are not informative beyond her duties in the White House.

Robin letters, Calvin Coolidge Memorial Foundation. Letters began in 1915 but were not kept until 1920, when Grace Coolidge's increasing prominence as her husband moved toward the vice presidency and presidency persuaded Anna Nickerson to keep copies. Mrs. Coolidge wrote regularly, and her last letter was January 26, 1957.

Ishbel Ross papers, Library of Congress. The papers have no trace of correspondence with personalities of the Coolidge era, nor of drafts and other papers relating to composition of her biography of Grace Coolidge.

Maude Trumbull papers, Calvin Coolidge Memorial Foundation. The mother-in-law of John Coolidge soon was writing to Mrs. Coolidge and vice versa, and the collection shows visits of Mrs. Coolidge to the house of Governor and Mrs. Trumbull.

NEWSPAPERS

The best recourse for newspaper stories about Grace Coolidge is the University Microfilms system by which the Ann Arbor, Michigan, company has not merely indexed but made available printouts of Mrs. Coolidge's activities, as noted in the *New York Times, Washington Post, Chicago Tribune,* and *Los Angeles Times.* Identifications may be made by topics or by numbers of mentions of individual names. The Annie M. Hannay collection of clippings, Forbes Library, twenty-seven volumes, includes newspapers not indexed by University Microfilms, but is without large advantage because the compiler, Hannay, discovered few stories not already used by the major papers.

INDEX

Academy of Music (Northampton), 88, 145–146
Adams, Abigail, 58
Adams, Florence B., 121–122, 132–141, 143, 148, 150, 153
Adams, Jane, 132, 134, 148, 153
Adams, John, 58
Adams House (Boston), 41, 44, 50
Adventures in Autobiography (book), by H. G. Wells, 150
African Americans, 50
African Violet Society of America, 151
Allies' Inn (Washington, D.C.), 134
American (magazine), 12
American Asylum for the Education and Instruction of the Deaf and Dumb (Hartford), 18
American Baseball League, 35, 90
American Federation of Labor, 40–41
American Horticultural Society, 91–92
American Legion, 129
American Revolution, 3–4
American Shakespeare Foundation, 92–93
American Women's Club (London), 137
Amherst College, 20, 36, 39, 82, 85, 94, 150
Andrews, Adolphus, 86
Andrews, Adolphus, Mrs., 81
Arthur, Chester A., 66
Associated Press, 134
Austria, 136

Bacher, Edward, 36–37
Barren, Clarence W., 73, 118

Barrett family, 5, 88. *See also* Goodhue, Lemira
Belgium, 137
Bell, Alexander Graham, 19
Bell, Melville, 39
Bizet, Georges, 81
Blair-Lee House, 69
Bloedorn, Walter, 114
Bloom, Vera, 75–76
Bok, Edward W., 120
Boone, Helen, 144
Boone, Joel T., 22, 28, 31, 33–34, 66, 84, 86, 97, 99–101, 104, 106–109, 111, 113–114, 116, 127, 132–133, 136, 141–142, 153
Boston and Maine Railroad, 37
Boston police strike, 40–41
Boston Red Sox, 89–91
Boston University, 86
Brahms, Johannes, 81
Braidwood, Thomas, 19
Bremen (liner), 136–137, 139
Britton, Nanna P., 62
Brown, Richard, 36–37
Brown, Stephen, 36–37
Bryan, William Jennings, 139
Bukosky, John, 141, 145, 148
Burlington (steamer), 2
Burlington High School, 9
Butler, Nicholas Murray, 54–55
Butler, William H., 97

Calvin (movie house, Northampton), 145
Calvin Coolidge Memorial Room (Forbes Library), 152

"Calvin Coolidge Says," 126
Cambridge University, 136–137
Campfire Girls, 88–89
Capper, Arthur, 111–113
Carnivali, 81–82
Carr, Winifred, 85–86
Catholic church, 138
Catholic University, 89
Chamberlain, Neville, 136
Champlain Canal, 3
Charlton, Earle P., 118–119
Chase, Mary Ellen, 136–137, 151
Chicago Tribune, 68
Chickering Piano Company, 43, 82
Chopin, Frederic, 81
Christian Endeavor, 12
Christian Science church, 128
Christy, Howard Chandler, 86–87, 151
Cilea, Francesco, 81–82
Civil War, 1–2, 13
Clark, Charles E., 4
Clark, Edward T., 55–56, 130
Clarke, John, 19
Clarke School for the Deaf, 17–21, 25, 33, 69, 73, 118–119, 144–146, 150
Cleveland, Frances Folsom. *See* Preston, Frances Folsom
Cleveland, Grover, 8–9, 62, 67
Cleveland Indians, 90–91
Coast Guard, 83
Coleman, Joe, 90–91
Collins, Joseph D., 150
Columbian Exposition (1893), 74
Columbia University, 54
Comey, Morris L., 127
Comey, Morris L., Mrs., 127
Congregational Church, 1
Congress, 54, 64, 67–68
Constitutional Convention (Philadelphia, 1787), 4
Copley-Plaza Hotel (Boston), 42
Corelli, Archangelo, 81
Cosmopolitan (magazine), 64
Coolidge, Abigail, 29, 104, 125–126

Coolidge, Calvin
    The Beeches, the Notch "lean-to," 126–128
    courtship of Grace Goodhue, 20–26
    decline and death, 128–131
    family, 96–120
    Mayflower, 79–80
    Northampton again, 122–125
    Northampton and Boston, 27–44
    receptions, 82–85
    vice president, 44–56
    writings, 125–126
Coolidge, Calvin Jr. (son), 12, 27, 35–36, 42, 45, 48–49, 96–97, 100–104, 106–107, 134, 141, 153
Coolidge, Cynthia (granddaughter), 136, 138, 152
Coolidge, Florence Trumbull (daughter-in-law), 116–117, 125, 127, 129, 136, 148, 152
Coolidge, Grace (wife)
    adjustment to being first lady, 57–70
    charm, 72–76
    conclusion, 152–154
    courtship, 20–26
    early years, 1–19
    family, 96–120
    fashion leader, 71–72
    later years, 143–152
    Northampton, 27–46
    public events, 77–95
    together, alone, 121–142
    vice presidency, 46–56
Coolidge and Hemenway, 145
Coolidge, John (father of Calvin), 22–23, 34–36, 39, 42, 44–45, 104–106, 127–128
Coolidge, John (son), 12, 27, 34–36, 39, 42, 48–49, 94, 96–97, 100–102, 106–107, 110, 116–118, 127, 129, 132–134, 136, 138, 148, 152–153
Coolidge, Lydia (granddaughter), 152

Coolidge, Sarah Almeda Brewer (grandmother), 22–23, 34, 130
Coolidge, Victoria (mother), 20, 104, 125–127
Coupal, James F., 114
Cram, Ralph Adams, 107
Crane, Winthrop Murray, 39, 43
Cronin, Joe, 91
Cuba, 4
Curtis, Charles, 54
Curtis, Cyrus H., 118–119
Czechoslovakia, 136

Daughters of the American Revolution, 88, 146
Davies, Marion, 124
Davis, John W., 105
Dawes, Charles G., 54, 90
Dawes, Charles G., Mrs., 91–92
Delano, William Adams, 68–69
Denmark, 139
Derieux, James C., 66
Dewey, George, 4
Dickens, Paul, 114
Doherty, Henry L., 118–119
Dollar Steamship Company, 125

Edwards Congregational Church (Northampton), 12, 90–91, 102, 125, 146–147, 153–154
Eighteenth Amendment, 46, 80–81
Eisenhower, Dwight D., 1
Épee, Abbé de l', 18
Episcopal church (Northampton), 132
Ethiopia, 137
Europa (liner), 139

Fairbanks, Douglas, 125
Farley, James A., 139
First Baptist Church (Burlington), 2
First Church Congregational (Burlington), 2
First Congregational Church (Washington, D.C.), 82, 94

Fitzgerald, F. Scott, 151
Flotow, Friedrich, 81–82
Folger Shakespeare Library (Washington, D.C.), 134
Forbes Library, 146. *See also* Calvin Coolidge Memorial Room
Ford, Henry, 129
Ford, Henry, Mrs., 129
Fort Benning (Georgia), 89
Fort Ticonderoga, 1
France, 136–138
Franklin, Benjamin, 82
Frost, Robert, 3

Gale, Ivah W., 11–12, 14–15, 24–25, 33–34, 128–129, 136, 148, 151–153
Gallaudet, Edward, 18–19
Gallaudet, Thomas, 18
Gallaudet University, 18–19
Gambel, Hugh C., 92
Ganz, Rudolph, 81
Garbo, Greta, 145
Garman, Charles E., 20, 36, 150
George Washington University, 86
Germany, 46, 122, 136, 139
Gibson, Charles Dana, 14
Gigli, Beniamino, 81–82
Gilbert and Sullivan, 82
Girl Scouts, 75, 88–89
Gold Star Mothers, 74
Gompers, Samuel, 40–41
Gone with the Wind (book), by Margaret Mitchell, 150
Good Housekeeping (magazine), 12, 23, 26, 28
Goodhue, Andrew I., 5–11, 15, 24, 34, 42, 54, 88, 121–122, 153
Goodhue, Lemira, 5–9, 18, 24–25, 31, 54, 116, 153
Goodhue family, 2, 4–5
Gounod, Charles, 81
"Gradatim" (poem), by Josiah G. Holland, 42–43
Graf Zeppelin, 68

Grant, Ulysses S., 2, 82
Grant, Ulysses S. III, 69
Great Britain, 136–137
Great Depression, 129, 134
Greece, 137
Grove Park Inn (Asheville, N.C.), 46

Hagner, Isabelle, 59
Hale, Raleigh P., 93
Haley, James, 97, 101–102, 105, 110–111
Hamilton, Alexander, 62
Harding, Florence, 54–55, 57, 61–63,
      65, 73, 78–79
Harding, Warren G., 43, 46, 54–55, 61–
      62, 65, 79, 82–83, 97
Harkness, Edward S., 118–119
Harlan, John M., 63
Harlan, Laura, 63, 92
Harris, Stanley, 91
Harvard University, 39
Haydn, Joseph, 82
Hearst, William Randolph, 123–125
Hemenway, Ralph W., 123
Henderson, John B., Mrs., 54–55
Hills, Jack, 36, 116, 132
Hills, Reuben B., 36, 116, 132
Hills, Therese, 36–37, 48, 50, 53–54,
      98, 116, 122, 125, 128, 132–133
Hitler, Adolf, 136
Holland, Josiah G., 42–43
Homer, Louise, 82
Hoover, Herbert, 29, 64, 80, 97, 112,
      116, 126, 129–130
Hoover, Irwin H. (Ike), 66
Hoover, Lou Henry, 89
House, Edward M., 60–61
Howells, William Dean, 1
Hubbard, Gardiner Greene, 19, 119

Italy, 137

Jackson, Andrew, 18–19, 82
Jaffray, Elizabeth, 64–66. See also *Se-
      crets of the White House* (book)

James, Marquis, 61
Japan, 60, 144
Johns Hopkins University, 61, 114
Johnson, Hiram, 43–44

Keller, Helen, 75
Kendall, Amos, 18–19
Kennedy, John J., 38
Keyes, Frances Parkinson, 73, 75, 151
Keyes, Henry, 73
King, Henry Churchill, 86
Kingsley, Darwin P., 86
Kirby, Fred M., 118–119
Kreisler, Fritz, 81
Kundred, A. E., 92

Lafayette, Marquis du, 13
Lake Champlain Yacht Club (Bur-
      lington), 4
Lakeside Inn (Mount Dora, Fl.), 123
Lalo, Edward, 81–82
Landon, Alfred, 138–139
Lane, William H., 8
Laszlo de Lombos, Alexius de, 86
League of Nations, 46, 61
Lenroot, Irvine L., 43
Lewis, John L., 148
Library of Congress, 28, 61
*Life and Times of William Howard
      Taft* (book), by Henry F. Pringle,
      150–151
Lincoln Memorial (Washington,
      D.C.), 86
Liszt, Franz, 81
Lodge, Henry Cabot, 30, 39, 43–44,
      61, 78, 103–104
Longfellow, Henry W., 16
Longworth, Alice Roosevelt, 91–92.
      See also Roosevelt, Alice
Longworth, Nicholas, 91–92
Lorimer, George Horace, Mrs., 67

Madison, Dolley, 58
Manila Bay (battle), 4

Mann, Horace, 18
Margaret, Princess, 149
Marine Band, 62, 87, 92
Marine Corps, 83, 136
Marine Orchestra, 83–84
Marion (Ohio) Star (newspaper), 73
Marshall, Lois Kinsey, 49–50, 52–53
Marshall, Thomas W., 49–50, 56
Masonic Hall (Burlington), 15
Massenet, Jules, 82
Mayflower (yacht), 22, 79–81, 86, 89,
    106, 120, 134
McCamant, Wallace, 44
McCormick, A. H., 26
McCracken, Henry Noble, 127
McKim, Charles E., 59, 66–68, 79
McKim, Mead and White, 59
McKinley, William, 2, 4, 58, 64
Medinus, Grace G., 127, 130
Mellon, Andrew W., 118–119
Mercersburg Academy, 48–49, 97–
    100, 107
Merrill, Christine, 75
Merrill, Robert, 75
Methodist Episcopal Church (Bur-
    lington), 2, 10–11
Metropolitan Opera, 81–82
Morini, Erika, 81
Morrow, Dwight W., 137
Moszkowski, Moritz, 81
Mount Holyoke College, 98
Moussorgsky, Modest P., 81
Mussolini, Benito, 137
Mutiny on the Bounty (book), by
    Charles Nordhoff and James
    Norman Hall, 150

Nassau Hospital (Minneola, NY), 92
National Baseball League, 55
National Museum (Washington,
    D.C.), 134
National Recovery Act, 139
Navy Band, 80
New, Harry S., 129–130

New York Giants, 90
New York Times, 76, 85–86, 92–94,
    129, 135
Nichols, Dr., 25
Nickerson, Anna Robinson, 87
Nicolson, Harold, 137
Nielsen, William, 118
Nineteenth Amendment, 23–24
Northampton, Hotel, 145–146. *See
    also* Tavern, The
Northampton High School, 27, 144
North Carolina, University of, 119–120
Norwood Hotel (Northampton), 28–
    29

Oberlin College, 86
Oregon (battleship), 4
Owen, Ruth Bryan, 139

Paine, William A., 118–119
Paris Peace Conference (1919), 46, 60
Patterson, Robert M., Mrs., 68
Pearl Harbor, 144
Peiffer, Flora, 93
Phi Beta Kappa, 92–93
Philadelphia Athletics, 90–91
Philadelphia Orchestra, 53
Philippine Islands, 59
Phillips, Carrie, 62
Phillips, Frank, 118–119
Pi Beta Phi, 16–17, 86. *See also* robins
Pickford, Mary, 125, 135
Pierce, Aurora, 128
Pierson Company, F. R., 91
Poland, 136
Pollard, Sarah, 26
President Coolidge (liner), 125
President Hoover (liner), 125
Presidents and First Ladies (book), by
    Mary Randolph, 95
Preston, Frances Folsom, 67
Princeton University, 107
Printing and Engraving, Bureau of, 79
Proctor, Redfield, 4

Quantico (Marine base), 89

Rachmaninoff, Sergei, 81
Randolph, Mary, 63–64, 71, 82, 92–93.
　　See also *Presidents and First La-*
　　dies (book)
Rankin, Jeannette, 73–74
Raskob, John J., 118–119
Reckahn, Alice, 31, 37, 98, 123, 127
Red Cross, 52, 144
Representatives, House of, 73–74. *See*
　　also Congress
Republican National Convention
　　Chicago, 1920, 43–44
　　Kansas City, 1928, 116
Rescue (hospital ship), 136
Rethberg, Elizabeth, 82
Richardson, H. H., 146
Richardson, Sophia M., 31
Riley, Ellen A., 66
robins, 64, 136, 146, 148–149, 151
Rockefeller, John D., 91
Roosevelt, Alice, 59, 64, 74. *See also*
　　Longworth, Alice Roosevelt
Roosevelt, Edith, 58–60, 64, 66–67, 86
Roosevelt, Eleanor, 94–95
Roosevelt, Franklin D., 20, 46, 66, 68,
　　94, 129, 134, 139
Roosevelt, Theodore, 2, 57, 59, 79, 82–
　　83, 150–151
Ross, Ishbel, 33, 70, 121
Russo-Japanese War, 79

Sackville-West, Virginia, 137
Saint-Saens, Camille, 82
Salisbury, Frank A., 120
Sanders, Everett, 106, 133–134
San Simeon (castle), 113–114
Santiago (naval battle), 4
Saturday Evening Post, 67
Saturday Review of Literature, 151
Schubert, Franz, 82
Scott, Walter, 137

Scribner, Charles, 18
Second Church Congregational (Bur-
　　lington). *See* Unitarian Church
　　(Burlington)
Secret Service, 52, 71, 84, 109–110, 114
Secrets of the White House (book), by
　　Elizabeth Jaffray, 58, 64
Senate, 52–53, 76. *See also* Congress
Shakespeare Memorial Theater
　　(Stratford-on-Avon, Eng.), 92–93
Sheridan, Philip, 2
Sherrill, Clarence G., 87
Shoreham Hotel (Washington, D.C.),
　　78
Siam, 17
Smith, Alfred E., 109
Smith, Ira R. T., 104
Smith College, 28, 30, 86, 118, 121–122,
　　127, 134, 136–137, 143–145, 147,
　　151–152
Snow, Florence, 143, 153
Spain, 137
Spanish-American War, 23–24
Springfield Union (newspaper), 149
St. Joseph's, R. C., Church (Burling-
　　ton), 2
St. Mary's, R. C., Church (Burling-
　　ton), 2
St. Paul's Episcopal Church (Burling-
　　ton), 2
Starling, Edmund W., 71, 84, 104, 111,
　　116–117, 130–131
State, War and Navy Building (Wash-
　　ington, D.C.), 83
Steams, Emily, 33, 44–45, 56, 58–60,
　　78, 85, 95, 106, 111
Steams, Foster (son), 138
Steams, Frank W., 28, 35, 39, 41, 46,
　　48–50, 78, 94, 105, 130, 138
Stearns Department Store, R. A., 66,
　　138
Steinway and Sons, 77–78
Stevens, Ethel M., 24

Stover, Mrs., 93–94
Strauss, Johann, 81
Sturtevant, Mrs., 9
Sturtevant, Roy, 9, 13
Supreme Court, 53, 59, 63
Sutherland, Mary Elizabeth, 91
Swannanoa Country Club, 119
Sweden, 139
Switzerland, 138–139

Taft, Helen, 58–60, 64, 73, 79
Taft, William H., 59, 79, 84, 115, 150–151
Tarrytown (N.Y.) Horticultural Society, 91
Tartini, Giuseppe, 81
Tavern, The, 146–147
Taylor, Zachary, 58
Tchaikovsky, Pyotr I., 81
Third Congregational Church (Burlington), 2
Thomas, John Charles, 81–82
Thompson, William Boyce, 118–119
Tiffany, Louis, 59
Todd, Mary A., 88
Truman, Bess W., 32
Truman, Harry S., 69
Trumbull, Florence (daughter). *See* Coolidge, Florence Trumbull
Trumbull, John, 98
Trumbull, Maude, 128
Tumulty, Joseph P., 61

Underwood, Cornelia C., 9, 17
Underwood, Herbert W., 143–144
Underwood, Herbert W., Mrs., 143–144
Unitarian Church (Burlington), 2
United Mine Workers, 148
United Press, 134

Van Buren, Martin, 2
Vassar College, 127
Verdi, Giuseppe, 81–82

Vermont, University of, 2–3, 12–18, 86, 92–93, 144–145, 152
Vermont Fish and Game League, 2
Vermont II (steamer), 2, 4, 131
Versailles, Treaty of, 46, 136
Veterans' Bureau, 66
Virginia, University of, 119–120

Wall Street Journal, 118
Walter Reed Hospital, 62, 102
Wambsganss, Bill, 90–91
War Department, 74–75
Washington, George, 80, 82
Washington, Martha, 58, 87
Washington College Woman's Club (Washington, D.C.), 88
Washington Navy Yard, 79–80
Washington Post, 71–72, 76, 135
Washington Senators, 90–91, 150
Waubanakee Golf Club (Burlington), 4
Waves (Women Accepted for Volunteer Emergency Service), 143–145
Wayside Inn, 129
Weir, Robert B., 19–20, 22, 24
Wicker Memorial Park (Hammond, Ind.), 93
Willard Hotel (Washington, D.C.), 50, 52–53, 55, 57
Wilson, Edith, 60–61, 65, 73
Wilson, Ellen, 60, 73
Wilson, Woodrow, 41, 46, 49, 56, 61–62, 79, 83
Windsor, Duchess of, 149
Winship, Bianton, 139
Winship, North, Mrs., 139
Wister, Owen, 7
Wolf, Hugo, 81
Woman's World Fair (Chicago, 1925), 74
Women Accepted for Volunteer Emergency Service. *See* Waves
Women's Universal Alliance, 75–76

Work, Hubert, 97
World War I, 1, 1, 10, 28, 46, 52, 60–61, 70, 107, 109–110, 140
World War II, 1, 125, 143–144, 149

Yale, Caroline, 18, 119
Yale, John Lyman, 18
Yale, June, 18
Young, Hugh, 61, 114